We often try to stand up straight all by ourselves. But we actually need to lean on someone else. Deb Burma beautifully describes how we are made to lean on Jesus. She has us lean in to study the wonderful promises of God's care. She then leans us back to apply this strength in our daily lives. As with all her writing, Deb shares the adventures and challenges of her life and her need to lean on God and others. Stop trying to stand alone. Lean on Jesus for all His strength.

DANIEL PAAVOLA, professor of theology at Concordia University Wisconsin

Success often comes when we simplify, streamline, and break things down. That's what Deb Burma offers through one word—*leaning*. In her latest study, *Leaning on Jesus: A Study of God's Strength*, Deb takes Proverbs 3:5—"Do not lean on your own understanding"—and creates an outstanding Bible study for individuals and groups. Sprinkled with endearing personal stories and saturated with Scripture, this book encourages the posture of "leaning, leaning, leaning on the everlasting arms" of Jesus, whose strength is always enough. I highly recommend this study!

REED LESSING, professor of Old Testament and director of the Center for Biblical Studies, Concordia University, St. Paul

Anyone who has met Deb knows her love of people. As she travels throughout the country, inspiring women, she takes time to listen, lean in, and let each conversation linger in her heart. Her new study, *Leaning on Jesus*, combines her passion for people and love of Jesus. You may find yourself listening to, lingering with, and leaning on Jesus more—and leaning in to love and learn from the people God places in your path too. With each of Deb's books, I sink into her words as an irresistible armchair to sit and rest and remember what matters.

LINDSAY HAUSCH, author and blogger

Deb does a wonderful job of giving practical situations and tools that direct us to Christ. As I read through this book, I was moved to examine my own life and reminded to lean back and reflect and to lean in and learn from Jesus. This is a great study for anyone in any part of her life.

REHEMA KAVUGHA, director of Synod relations, Lutheran Church Extension Fund

I leaned in immediately. Through personal stories told with humor and heart, the words in these pages will invite you to explore God's Word. Throughout this study, Deb emphasizes our dependence on our Savior in the most delightful way. She assures her readers that we are invited by our Lord to lean on Him and that we will find strength in and through our Savior. What a joy to lean on His promises in the pages of this book and throughout our lives. Deb Burma brings her readers another great resource with practical applications.

DEBBIE LARSON, Lutheran Women's Missionary League president, 2019–2023

This is an incredible study focusing on our need to rely on God in all circumstances. Deb does an incredible job of drawing the reader in, making it very personal. She encourages the reader to remember that God is always by our side, walking with us—something we all need daily reminding of. The study was very personal for me—something I really needed.

ANNE HARTMAN, mother and LWML volunteer, Eau Claire, Wisconsin

Each chapter of this book meets me where I am in my daily struggles and triumphs. It gives daily reminders of who God is: my hiding place, deliverer, Savior, and Lord. *Leaning on Jesus* reminds me that I don't go through life alone, but Christ is always with me. Each day's study shows biblical truths of how God works through my posture of leaning on Him.

CAMI HAMER, director of Christian education, Peace Lutheran Church, Columbus, Nebraska

Surrounded by the world's message that "we are enough just as we are," Deb Burma's *Leaning on Jesus* reminds us that "apart from [Him we] can do nothing" (John 15:5). This study manages to densely pack scriptural encouragement and helpful insights into bite-size readings perfect for anyone who wants to lean into God's Word but finds herself in a busy season of life. This Bible study will point the reader back to Jesus over and over again, reminding us that our God can handle it all—our sin, weakness, and discouragement—meeting us where we are and bringing us the comfort and peace won for us on the cross.

CHRISTA PETZOLD, author of *Gathered by Christ: The Overlooked Gift of Church*

Leaning on JESUS

A STUDY OF GOD'S STRENGTH

DEB BURMA

CONCORDIA PUBLISHING HOUSE · SAINT LOUIS

Published by Concordia Publishing House
3558 S. Jefferson Ave., St. Louis, MO 63118-3968
1-800-325-3040 · cph.org

Manufactured in Dongguan City, China/064630/340883

1 2 3 4 5 6 7 8 9 10   32 31 30 29 28 27 26 25 24 23

Dedicated to my family

Cory

Chris & Megan

Courtney & Aaron

Cameron & Katherine

We've done a lot of leaning together, haven't we?

May you see in me what I witness in you: God-given trust that leads you to lean on Jesus always.

Let's keep leaning on one another as we rest in His embrace.

To God be the glory!

CONTENTS

Introduction   10

How to Use This Study   12

WEEK 1: The Only One Worthy of Our Full Weight

DAY ONE   15

DAY TWO   19

DAY THREE   24

DAY FOUR   29

DAY FIVE   34

WEEK 2: Leaning on Jesus When We Don't Understand

DAY ONE   43

DAY TWO   47

DAY THREE   51

DAY FOUR   55

DAY FIVE   60

WEEK 3: Leaning on Jesus When We're Weary

DAY ONE   69

DAY TWO   74

DAY THREE   77

DAY FOUR   81

DAY FIVE   86

WEEK 4: Leaning on Jesus When We're Weak

DAY ONE   93

DAY TWO   97

DAY THREE   101

DAY FOUR   105

DAY FIVE   108

WEEK 5: Leaning on Jesus When We Need Comfort

DAY ONE	117
DAY TWO	121
DAY THREE	125
DAY FOUR	128
DAY FIVE	133

WEEK 6: Leaning In to Listen and Learn → To Lead Well

DAY ONE	141
DAY TWO	145
DAY THREE	149
DAY FOUR	153
DAY FIVE	156

WEEK 7: Leaning on Jesus Together

DAY ONE	163
DAY TWO	166
DAY THREE	170
DAY FOUR	174
DAY FIVE	177

WEEK 8: Leaning on One Another

DAY ONE	183
DAY TWO	186
DAY THREE	189
DAY FOUR	193
DAY FIVE	197

Daily Session Answers — **204**

Endnotes — **218**

Proper POSTURE

How's your posture? (You sat up a little straighter just now, didn't you?) Were you slouching? Slumping? In need of a little lumbar support? (Now you're checking your spine.) As a child, maybe you were told to sit straight, stand tall, keep your chin up, and pick up your feet. While this is healthy advice for a good stance, I'd like to propose a different posture—*leaning.*

Our culture encourages independence and promotes self-empowerment. We're taught to stand on our own two feet, to proverbially "pull ourselves up by our bootstraps." Any number of memes, blog posts, videos, and the like are filled with self-affirming words we can recite to ourselves.

While there's nothing wrong with putting our best foot forward, what happens if that foot fails us? What if we trip and fall over said obstacle? When we realize that sometimes we're just plain weak and weary? Or when we lack wisdom, direction, or understanding? What then?

While society encourages an independent posture, what could it look like to live out (and promote) a dependent posture of leaning?

First, leaning on Jesus.

Then, leaning on one another.

We weren't meant to go it alone, let alone lean on ourselves (as if that were even possible). As we lean ON and lean IN to the only One worthy of our full weight, we will see that Jesus alone provides true empowerment. We will recognize our complete dependence on Him, for He alone is our source of salvation and strength. He possesses perfect understanding. He provides comfort as no one else can. By God's grace, we can respond to His call to lean on one another too.

As we work through this book, we will learn to surrender our situations to our Savior, relinquish our control to Him, and rest in His all-powerful arms. We receive all we need as we lean on Jesus.

When and why do we lean on Jesus? (And what happens when we do?)

How does leaning on Jesus impact our faith and our witness for Him as we lean *in* to learn and lean *forward* with anticipation? As we trust Him with all our heart and lean *not* on our own understanding (see Proverbs 3:5)?

In this book, we'll examine what Scripture says about leaning on the Lord and on one another. We will unpack promises found across God's Word and fulfilled in Christ.

We were called to be a people who lean on Jesus. Let's learn more.

BEHIND THE SCENES

When the imagery of leaning wouldn't leave me alone, I began writing an email to my publicist, Elizabeth, sharing the Scripture behind the inspiration and allowing my thoughts to flow. While I was typing, my phone chimed. I read the text and smiled as I replied. Returning to my email, I wrote, "A friend just texted me a prayer request. She doesn't know I'm writing this to you (or even that I have this idea), but she said: 'It's more than we can handle on our own. We have to lean on our heavenly Father; He's our comfort and protector!'"

We need Jesus. All. The. Time. But sometimes our need seems more acute. While writing this book, I led workshops, retreats, and small-group sessions. I asked a lot of people when they most recognized their need to lean on Jesus. I inquired via social media too. While each person's reasons and stories are unique, there were consistent themes.

We lean on Jesus

Daily, letting go of control and giving it all to God

During difficult times when we can't make sense of anything

For strength when we feel inadequate, anxious, or afraid

For comfort in times of distress and loneliness, trials and pain, loss and grief

During life transitions and major decisions

During medical tests, treatments, and the care of loved ones

Women across the country shared their hearts with me:

"I cannot imagine going through this situation without our Lord to lean on."

"I delight in knowing that I can climb up into my Father's lap."

"His sheltering arms are holding me."

"Every day I need to lean on Him for daily strength and love."

"He holds [my kids] as He holds me."

"The hardest times when I had to lean on Jesus were the best times in my life."

Our need to lean on Jesus isn't limited to times of struggle or sorrow.

We have a continuous need—in joy and in suffering—to rely on Him, to receive His help and hope.

Are you leaning on Jesus today? Did you know you can bring everything to Him, lay it at His feet, and rest in His arms? He hears your every thought; He knows what's on your heart. He sees what lies ahead, and He is present with you now. Lean on Him.

HOW TO USE THIS STUDY

Leaning on Jesus is flexible, so it may be used for personal Bible study or with a group. There are eight weeks and each is divided into five days or sessions for study, forty sessions total. I pray this format encourages you toward daily study and devotion time. Plan for twenty to thirty minutes to complete each daily session. However, if your schedule doesn't allow for daily study, you may save your study time for one or two longer sittings each week.

I encourage you to open with prayer, whether you're alone, preparing for group study, or gathered with your group. Ask the Lord to guide and grow you through the Word, by the power of the Holy Spirit. Ask Him to hold you in His embrace as you lean on Him.

Then, ask yourself how and where you will lean in to learn, to receive rest and refreshment from the Lord. Give yourself grace and enjoy this book in a way that works for you.

As you read and study, highlight or circle what stands out to you in each session. Make it personal: what speaks to you? You can bring that to the group discussion.

In each session, you'll find two types of questions:

Lean Back for personal reflection. Take time to pause and ponder these questions. Consider which ones to share as you gather with others and engage in group discussion.

Lean In to go straight to Scripture (answers begin on page 204; I highly recommend that you access them). Lean in to learn as you respond to questions and apply them to daily life.

In addition to the questions, set to the side are daily *Leaning-In Action* activities tied to the topic of the day, prompting you to apply it in your life.

There is no one way or right way to complete *Leaning on Jesus.* May God's guidance lead you to it and His grace carry you through it as you lean on Him. Allow the Holy Spirit to work through the Word as you "trust in the LORD with all your heart, and do not lean on your own understanding" (Proverbs 3:5).

Leaning on Jesus with you,

Deb Burma

The Only One
WORTHY OF OUR
FULL WEIGHT

Leaning on Jesus. Everywhere I turned, I kept hearing this message. Before long, I was talking about *leaning* at a women's event, on a podcast, and in social media posts. While I was developing this idea into a retreat topic, my friend, speaker and humorist Jan Struck, reached out to me with a clever invitation: "The women of my church would like to know what topic you're currently creating that's half-baked. (You know, doughy in the middle.) We'd love to have you fly down here to speak, and we'll help you do some further baking at the retreat!" Thrilled with her request, I agreed to do some "baking" in sunny Florida. All weekend, we sought the Lord's wisdom, unpacked many of His promises, and reminded one another of our need to lean fully on Jesus. We even crafted printed pillows that read "Lean on Jesus."

Thrilled with the women's responses and praising God for a successful retreat, Jan and I followed the weekend with some extended-stay Florida fun. Monday morning, Jan ran an errand while I prepared for the day. With my curling iron in one hand, I leaned toward the mirror and reached for the iron with my other hand to steady it. But instead of the handgrip, I touched the hot barrel. I flinched, my hand jerked, and the barrel touched my eyeball. I screamed in pain as my eyeball burned and tears streamed out. I couldn't see anything but light with my injured eye. I ran down the hall, reached for the refrigerator, and frantically grabbed ice to ease the searing pain.

Life changed in the blink of an eye. All was well . . . until it wasn't. Thank the Lord, Jan soon walked through the door, whisked me up in a comical sort of panic, and rushed me to the emergency room. Pain worsened when I held the other eye open, so I kept both eyes closed. When we arrived, I leaned heavily on my friend as we made our way into the ER. One of the security agents overheard my lament that my ice had melted and the pain was increasing. The security agent hollered, "Don't put ice on a burn! It will make it worse!" In unison, Jan and I gasped, worrying that we had aggravated the injury even more. Later, while we waited for a room, a nurse came by with a cart full of medical supplies. She saw me rocking back and forth in pain and asked if I would like ice. Jan quickly exclaimed, "We were told that would make it worse!" The nurse scowled, "Who told you that?" Jan sheepishly admitted, "A security guard." Taken aback, the nurse said, "You took medical advice from security personnel?!" I humbly accepted more ice.

Meanwhile, scenarios ran through my mind: *What if I have permanent vision loss? Will I be able to continue this and other ministry pursuits? How will I explain this to my family?* At almost the same time, a wave of peace washed over me as I remembered that I am safely in Jesus' grip, and He provides soothing relief of another kind. I am in Jesus' presence, His knowledge, and His care. He will use this for good. He even provided the ER staff and Jan for physical care and bouts of unexpected laughter amid the pain.

The ER doctor's diagnosis—corneal abrasion—came with a healthy dose of encouragement: I would regain full vision. Praise the Lord! When we left, I was sporting a black pirate patch complete with an elastic band around my head. We made our way to a pharmacy to fill my prescription and found ourselves pausing in the parking lot. Filled with emotion, I told Jan, "We can talk a lot about leaning on Jesus, and that sounds great when all is well, but what happens when all is—quite suddenly—not well? Do we panic? Are we distracted by wayward messages? Where do we go to seek real help? And do we recognize God's work through another person who holds us up as we lean heavily on her?"

We hugging and laughing amid tears, and I again put my full weight on Jan as we walked through the store. Suddenly—wham! Jan led me straight into a giant soft drink display! She called out to anyone within earshot, "My friend is leaning on me, and this is what I lead her into!" Then to me, she said, "I am not worthy of your full weight, Deb!" More laughter. More tears. No harm done. But Jan was right. Only Jesus can take our full weight. He bore the full weight of our sins at the cross and freed us from them. Not only can we lean on Him in times of trouble but also every day for every need—when all is well and when it isn't.

LEAN BACK:

All was well . . . until it wasn't. When did something change in the blink of an eye for you? How did you respond?

Have you fallen for faulty advice? What or who led you to the truth via correction or by example?

Maybe the posture of leaning on Jesus is new to you. What other words further define what *lean* means in this context? When we respond to His grace, recognize our dependence on Him, and seek His lead in our lives, we may use words like these:

Follow	*Trust*
Listen	*Rely*
Need	*Learn*

LEAN IN #1: Which one of these words helps you unpack the imagery of leaning? How would you combine these words to define *lean* in this context? Let these verses give you a starting place for the consideration of each word: Matthew 16:24; Luke 10:39; Matthew 6:8; Psalm 28:7; Isaiah 50:10; John 6:45. You will find these descriptors repeatedly throughout this study.

JESUS' LITTLE LAMB

My bashful twin toddlers often clung to me, hugging my leg or hiding behind me whenever someone new approached. Their tight attachment assured me they wouldn't wander away, but sometimes mere movement was difficult, so I learned to lift them simultaneously (requiring deep knee bends in a quad-strengthening squat!). Like countless other mothers, I scooped them up and carried them in my arms. Snuggled against my chest, they received reassurance that they were safe.

Isaiah 40:10–11 provides the imagery of our Lord with His powerful arm. He is strong to save and tender to scoop us up and carry us as a shepherd holds his lambs close to his heart. "He will tend His flock like a shepherd; He will gather the lambs in His arms; He will carry them in His bosom" (v. 11).

This shows Jesus as the Good Shepherd, watching over His precious sheep who surround Him. You have likely seen paintings depicting Jesus holding a lamb in His arms or carrying one over His shoulders. The entire flock receives the Shepherd's care

LEANING-IN ACTION: Have you experienced peace amid tumult? Apply these truths, then share your story:

Jesus has you in His grip.

Nothing happens apart from His presence, knowledge, and care.

He will use this for good, even if you cannot imagine that is possible.

He may provide for you through other people.

LEANING-IN
ACTION:
Meditate on
a sacred song
about sheep or
the Shepherd.
What words reso-
nate with you?
Make a joyful
noise and lift
your voice to the
Good Shepherd.

as they walk next to Him, follow His lead, or rest in His arms. Nothing can separate the Shepherd from His flock.

Whenever we approach something that scares us, we may hide in His embrace, confident that we won't encounter danger without the protection of His strong arms around us. We are safely in the fold of the Good Shepherd. Perhaps you hummed this children's song as soon as you saw today's title: "I Am Jesus' Little Lamb."

I am Jesus' little lamb,

Ever glad at heart I am;

For my Shepherd gently guides me,

Knows my need and well provides me,

Loves me ev'ry day the same,

Even calls me by my name.

He leads and guides me. He knows my needs and provides for them. He loves me always and calls me by name. The last lines of the third stanza catch in my throat:

He shall fold me to His breast,

There within His arms to rest.[1]

LEAN IN #2: How do the last two lines of this song relate directly to Isaiah 40:11?

LEAN IN #3: Connect lines from the first stanza (above) of "I Am Jesus' Little Lamb" to promises found in these passages, citing the Scripture reference beside the line of the song: Psalm 23:1–3; Isaiah 43:1; Jeremiah 31:3; John 10:3; John 10:14; 1 John 3:1a.

Needy

Not one to be outdone by his big brother or sister, my youngest child would lean against my legs and cling to the hem of my shirt with one hand while straining up with the other. His refrain still rings in my ears: "I need you, Mama! I neeeeeed you!" And what were those needs? Comfort, security, and love. A few times, it was fear that led him to lean on me. More often it was fatigue and the recognition of his need for me.

With a tender heart for all of my toddlers, I carried them countless times. And when they outgrew my arms, I nurtured and protected them throughout their growing years. That's what a parent does. Small children are helpless on their own; they fully rely on their parents for every need. As children grow, they exert independence and often erroneously think they can go it alone before they're ready. "I do it myself!" my children exclaimed many times, only to realize they still needed my help. But they were learning as they grew. And they knew they could look to their parents for guidance and support—for a strong arm to reach down and lift them up.

Jesus' strong arms held little children, "even infants," according to Luke's account (Luke 18:15). Matthew adds that people brought children to Jesus so He might pray for them (Matthew 19:13) as He opened His arms wide, drew them near, and held them in His embrace. Note the details of Mark's account:

> And [the people] were bringing children to Him that He might touch them, and the disciples rebuked them. But when Jesus saw it, He was indignant and said to them, "Let the children come to Me; do not hinder them, for to such belongs the kingdom of God. Truly, I say to you, whoever does not receive the kingdom of God like a child shall not enter it." And He took them in His arms and blessed them, laying His hands on them. (Mark 10:13–16)

LEAN IN #1: Look at the last sentence in Mark's passage again. What was Jesus' posture and response toward the children? What do you think He meant when He spoke of receiving the kingdom of God like a child in order to enter it?

I can still feel my mom's soft shoulder against my face as I sleepily leaned on her arm while Dad drove the long road home to the farm. I wouldn't have been able to hold my head up, in more ways than this, without the continual comfort and support provided by my parents.

A growing child gains gradual independence. A healthy level of autonomy is necessary for us to become responsible, mature adults who can take care of ourselves apart from our parents' constant care. That's where our lives as children of God differ from our lives as grown children of our parents. In fact, Jesus calls us to become like children—to humble ourselves like them (Matthew 18:3–4). We are completely dependent upon Him for salvation. Leaning on Jesus, we eagerly receive His embrace . . . and His grace. We humbly and freely receive all that we need—for now and eternity. Children of the heavenly Father, we continue to rely fully on Him, and we can expect unending opportunities for spiritual growth. Like the child with complete trust in a nurturing parent, we grow and thrive while still leaning on our heavenly Father for everything, knowing we cannot go or grow alone.

LEAN BACK:

Circle the word *need* in the verses below. Where your needs are concerned, what do you learn here about God? What does He promise to do or give? And what can you do regarding your needs? Highlight God's actions (or what He gives) and underline the actions you can take, by His grace.

Your father knows what you need before you ask Him. (Matthew 6:8)

In any and every circumstance, I have learned the secret of facing plenty and hunger, abundance and need. I can do all things through Him who strengthens me. . . . And my God will supply every need of yours according to His riches in glory in Christ Jesus. (Philippians 4:12–13, 19)

Let us then with confidence draw near to the throne of grace, that we may receive mercy and find grace to help in time of need. (Hebrews 4:16)

THE WONDERS OF HIS LOVE

I watched as seven-year-old Weslyn walked reverently down the aisle beside his daddy at the close of church service. With the long pole of the candle snuffer in hand, he followed his father's lead and covered each candle. His eyes filled with wonder as each flame was snuffed out. The last candle was the tallest, and Weslyn couldn't maneuver the long pole over it to snuff the flame. His dad walked across the chancel and placed his hands with Weslyn's on the pole. Together, they completed the task, turned, and recessed down the aisle. Weslyn beamed up at his dad, who met his gaze with a warm expression of fatherly love.

Jesus tells us the kingdom of heaven belongs to little children (Matthew 19:14). May we look at our lives in Christ the way Weslyn looked at his task: with eyes of wonder! May our eyes see the Lord's wonders all around us and the wonder of His love for us. "Show me the wonders of your great love, you who save by your right hand those who take refuge in you" (Psalm 17:7 NIV). I want to follow my heavenly Father's lead and wonder at what He enables me to do with His hand upon mine. May I look to Him, knowing His eyes are always on me. God expresses His great love for me in this: He saved me by His right hand when He sent His Son, my Savior. I receive refuge and rest in Him!

THE SHAPE OF LOVE

Love often takes shape in the form of a heart; some say it's a universal symbol for love. But what other shape does love take? What if we considered the thorns that were shaped into a crown and forced onto Jesus' head? Or the shape of the cross, on which our Savior died? More than a symbol, the cross was an instrument of torture and punishment, but on the day of Jesus' death, it was the place of

LEAN BACK:
Go ahead, take time right now to rest in Jesus. Read Psalm 136:1–9. Ponder the wonder of His steadfast love. Curl up in the arms of Jesus and snuggle into His embrace, relieved to rest there, fully reliant on Him.

complete sacrifice, once for all. It was love that led Him there. "God shows His love for us in that while we were still sinners, Christ died for us" (Romans 5:8). Love led Jesus to take our place, suffer and die for our sins, and rise again in victory over them. He secured our salvation by His sacrifice. Love led Him away from the empty tomb and home to the Father's house, where He prepares a place for us in eternity.

> **LEAN IN #2:** What shapes might you use to describe God's love in these passages?
>
> *John 3:16*
>
> *John 14:2–3*
>
> *Ephesians 3:16–19*

The God of all creation looks down on you and me with love: creative, redemptive, eternal love for us in Jesus. In awe, may we praise Him every day, across His creation, and with every posture we take! Whether we stand among the mountains or sit on a mound of snow. Whether we lift our hands as the sun rises over the beach or bow our heads before Him while the sun sets across the prairie. "From the rising of the sun to its setting, the name of the LORD is to be praised" (Psalm 113:3).

Nothing—not one thing—can ever separate you from God's love for you in Jesus, His Son and your Savior! His love is not something you've earned or even deserve. Nothing you do will cause Him to stop loving you, or to love you more than He already does, for that matter. His love for you is comprehensive, unconditional, and eternal.

LEAN IN #3: God inspired prophets and evangelists with images that help reveal the extent and wonders of His love. What images or comparisons regarding God's love appear in each passage?

Isaiah 49:15

Isaiah 62:5

Luke 13:34

Luke 15:11–32

John 15:13

LEAN BACK:

Read Romans 8:38–39, knowing that this promise is for you. In your words, summarize what you want to remember from this passage today.

The Domino Phenomenon OF DAILY LEANING

On my difficult days, I need Jesus. I cry out to Him. I ask others to pray. I look to His Word. I lean my full weight into Him. But you know what? I need Jesus just as much on my best days. Though if I'm honest, I forget that fact. When all is well in my world, I start to assume I have everything under control. But I need Him in the smoothly running daily things as much as ever. God is at work every day. I may not see how He is growing me, preparing me, and strengthening me for difficult days, but I trust that He is.

My friend and fellow author Lindsay Hausch viewed a YouTube video that gave her pause to consider the same thoughts. Dominoes of the same size placed on end create the well-known "domino effect" when one domino is pushed into the next, starting a chain reaction. This video, however, proves that "a domino can knock over another domino about one and a half times larger than itself. A chain of dominos of increasing size makes a kind of mechanical chain reaction that starts with a tiny push and knocks down an impressively large domino."[2] "As I was thinking of 'leaning on Jesus,'" Lindsay said, "this video came to mind. We lean on Jesus for small things day by day, and this multiplies into a lifetime of obedience, relationship, and God preparing us for the big moments in our lives!"[3] Watching this simple illustration and reviewing Lindsay's words, I recalled this quote from Corrie ten Boom: "Every experience God gives us, every person He puts in our lives is the perfect preparation for a future that only He can see."[4]

LEAN BACK:

For what small things will you lean on Jesus today? How do you think daily leaning impacts your relationship over a lifetime? How might your response of daily obedience prepare you for some impressively large moments in the future that only God can see?

WISE COUNSEL

I'm humbled by the knowledge that my Lord

never leaves my side. I don't go it alone, even when all is well. By His grace, I face plentiful sunshiny days. Even when it seems like I don't need it, He holds me close and gives me strength. I've learned these valuable lessons:

I can't go it alone with any lasting success.

Following my own logic, apart from His wisdom, will likely be my demise.

I don't know what's best for me apart from His counsel.

I still remember the wisdom provided by my first college advisor. I'd begun school with a major called "undeclared." (You've heard of it, yes?) And I think I would have sat complacently through endless general education classes were it not for his wise words that coaxed me in the direction I had been leaning but was too scared to go. Committing to "Communications" would mean a lot of writing and speaking classes. *Gulp. Was I ready for that?* While there were unexpected detours and surprising paths that followed, I'm thankful today for that advisor's guiding words that God used to lead me to this day.

Listen to advice and accept instruction, that you may gain wisdom in the future. (Proverbs 19:20)

By far the best counselor, advisor, or coach is the Lord God Himself. We may think we know what we want, but He knows far better what we need. We may stare at our situation, undeclared and complacent, failing to move forward on our own. In His perfect wisdom, He leads us by the Holy Spirit and coaxes us to lean on Him, to receive His instruction, to trust Him for a future only He can see. We can cling to every one of His promises, including this one in Psalm 32:8: "I will instruct you and teach you in the way you should go; I will counsel you with My eye upon you."

I've learned I need Jesus, my Counselor (Isaiah 9:6), for every decision I make. I humbly receive all I need from Him, and I respond by the Spirit's work in me.

♥ I want a willing heart to respond with discernment from the direction I receive in His Word.

LEANING-IN ACTION: Alone or with a group, stand dominoes in a pattern, then touch the front one to initiate the domino effect. What's the result of one tiny push? Apply this to the domino effect of daily leaning.

♥ I want focused eyes to see His path (including detours); I trust the Pathmaker, who guides me in all wisdom by His grace in Christ.

♥ I want listening ears to hear and a willingness to obey.

Sometimes He leads us by way of a godly mentor or a trusted Christian counselor with whom we can share our concerns and cares, a godly professional, specially trained to coach, comfort, and challenge us while sharing solid truth and wisdom from God's Word.

> **LEAN IN #1A:** Take a close look at 1 Corinthians 1:18–31 for guidance about wisdom. How is the wisdom of God contrasted with the wisdom of the world? Where is the wisdom of God found? What do we receive from "Christ . . . the wisdom of God" (v. 24) by faith?
>
> **1B:** How can we apply this passage to our daily decision-making? And what will lead every decision we make, by God's grace, in front of a watching world?

How may God advise you today? Do you need wisdom for a professional or personal decision? Direction for a relationship? Discernment for a tricky situation? Deliverance from a bad habit? Seek the counsel of the One who knows best and wants that for you. Talk to Him. Pour out your heart. Lean on Him. Whether all is *well* or all is *overwhelming*, recognize your continuous need and approach His throne of grace for "help in time of need" (Hebrews 4:16). Yes, every need, whether monumental or seemingly insignificant, because no need is too great or too small for the Lord's time, attention, and complete care.

I marvel that . . .

♥ The same Lord who created the heavens and the earth, who was and is and is to come—the Alpha and the Omega— is personally present and attentive to you and me.

❤ The One who formed every creature also formed you in your mother's womb; He knows the number of hairs on your head and stars in the sky.

❤ The triune God who transcends time is with you here and now and knows exactly what's on your heart (and on your schedule).

❤ The Lord who spoke the world into being also speaks to you today through His living and active Word.

❤ Jesus, the One who died for your sins and descended into hell, rose three days later, and ascended into heaven, resides in your heart by the Holy Spirit.

Does this sound like a God who can handle your very best days *and* your most difficult days? Is He worthy of your full weight? Amen. Can anything compare to Him? Nothing comes close.

LEAN IN #2: Look up each passage and note how God's creation or care is recorded there. What verse(s) stand out to you today and why?

> *Psalm 139:1–3, 13*
>
> *Isaiah 45:12*
>
> *Matthew 10:29–31*
>
> *Matthew 28:20b*
>
> *Acts 1:9–11*
>
> *1 Corinthians 15:3–4*
>
> *Colossians 1:27*
>
> *2 Timothy 3:16*
>
> *Hebrews 4:12a*
>
> *Revelation 1:8*

LEANING-IN ACTION: Do you need help with a decision or situation? An answer to a persistent question? Courage? Healing? Spend time in prayer, trusting that God hears your prayers in Jesus' name and responds according to His will.

LEAN BACK:

In the poetic praises of King David in Psalm 139, we learn a great deal about God's creation, knowledge, and care of us. Read verses 1–16. Using colored pencils or highlighters, mark God's demeanor or action toward us in one color. Then mark our actions and responses in another color. Which verses speak to His presence with us? His creation of us? His knowledge about us? Mark each one uniquely. Choose one verse that is especially meaningful to you today, whether it's been one of your best or most difficult days or somewhere between. Write this verse on a notecard and keep it with you as a regular reminder.

Declaration of DEPENDENCE

America was built, from its start, on a foundation of independence. We could say that we come by our independent spirit honestly. Countless Americans have fought for our freedom. We may find it difficult to consider ourselves dependent upon others, because we adopt the same independent American spirit that's passed down generation after generation.

While we may be independent from the reign of other nations, we are anything but independent. (Praise the Lord!) The One who created us also fought for our freedom from sin, won the victory for us at the cross, and sealed His victory at the empty tomb. We were adopted by the Father in Christ (Ephesians 1:5), the founder of our faith (Hebrews 12:2), who is perfecting that faith in us even now. He is rightly the sovereign and righteous ruler of our lives!

I would like to write my own "Declaration of Dependence," pronouncing my dependence upon the Lord. Better yet, I'll borrow the words of the psalmist in Psalm 71:

> **In You, O Lord, do I take refuge; let me never be put to shame! In Your righteousness deliver me and rescue me; incline Your ear to me, and save me! Be to me a rock of refuge, to which I may continually come; You have given the command to save me, for You are my rock and my fortress. Rescue me, O my God, from the hand of the wicked, from the grasp of the unjust and cruel man. For You, O Lord, are my hope, my trust, O Lord, from my youth. Upon You I have leaned from before my birth; You are He who took me from my mother's womb. My praise is continually of You. (Psalm 71:1–6)**

Like the psalmist, I can come before the Lord in praise and prayer. More than declaring, "In the Lord I take refuge," I can cry, "In You, O Lord, do I take refuge!" I praise Him for who He is and what He has already done for me. I lean fully on Him.

LEAN IN #1: Who does the psalmist say God is and what attributes does he mention?

The psalmist is confident in his request. Throughout his life, he has known the Lord by His faithfulness. More than saying, "I hope . . . I trust . . . ," the psalmist declares that the Lord IS his hope and trust; God is the object and the very definition of them.

> **LEAN IN #2:** Which words are repeated in this passage? How are they especially significant in the context of these verses? What two words are similar in meaning in this context? Finally, what words reveal the personal nature of this psalm?

The psalmist's cry for refuge implies that there is something or someone from whom he needs rescue. Although the wicked, the unjust, and the cruel endanger and threaten him, the psalmist knows that God is not just with him but so close as to incline His ear toward him. The Lord is so near, the psalmist can lean upon Him as he has done since before his birth. He makes his declaration of dependence right here! How sweet it is: dependence—from the womb—through past trials, into today, and for the future.

Penned thousands of years ago, the psalmist's requests are equally applicable to you and me. His cries could be ours. Even today, the wicked, unjust, and cruel threaten. Even today, we are compelled to lean on the Lord, the One who is our rock, fortress, and refuge.

Maybe you haven't known the Lord your entire life, but from the moment He first worked faith in your heart through the power of the Holy Spirit, in your Baptism or through the hearing of His Word, you have leaned on Him for your salvation. You have trusted in His saving grace. You have believed in Christ's sacrifice for the forgiveness of your sins.

A life of trust doesn't imply a life of ease that is free from threats, fears, or troubles. In the face of spiritual danger, however, the Lord is your trust. He is your

> rock—He is your strength. He supports your full weight.

> fortress—He surrounds you. He protects you on all sides.

> refuge—He guards you. He shelters you in safety.

"My praise is continually of You." Don't miss the psalmist's posture of praise. How could we respond to God's faithfulness—His strength, protection, and shelter—with anything less than our continual praise?! Amid every trouble, He is our hope and our trust. He alone is worthy of our unending praise and our full weight!

SUBTLE DECEPTION

Perhaps you have long since signed your Declaration of Dependence. You know you cannot go it alone, and you are happy to lean. Or maybe the pull to lean primarily on yourself is still strong. *On what or whom are you leaning?* We've already established the Lord to be worthy of our full weight. Why would we look to ourselves or to anything else? Unfortunately, we often do. Sometimes, we do it unintentionally; other times, accidentally; still other times, purposely and willfully.

LEAN BACK: It's important to note the psalmist's witness to our dependence on God in all things, at all times. Compare and contrast his acknowledgment of complete dependence upon the Lord with that of Christians today. When might believers of any generation deny God's involvement or necessity in every aspect of their lives? Why do you think that might be?

Early in my marriage, I fell for the subtly deceptive mantra "God helps those who help themselves." I was certain we should make a major decision in the direction I thought best. Doors kept slamming shut, but I pushed against them, thinking I was in control. *After all,* I thought, *I'm helping myself out here, taking the lead. Surely God will help make it happen!* Looking back, I praise God for His protection from what I thought I wanted. Much more accurate is the statement "God helps those who cannot help themselves."

LEANING-IN ACTION: Every time you lean back in a chair, in the driver's seat, or against a doorway or wall, let your posture remind you to ask, "How am I leaning on the Lord at this moment?"

When might we listen to, follow, or seek direction from alternate sources? Let me be clear: the Lord works through plenty of people and sources that provide godly wisdom, counsel, and instruction. But many other sources offer worldly wisdom, and it's all too easy to listen to them. Worldly wisdom is all around us, and often it's a soft sell. It sounds good. It may even make claims that sound like biblical truth but are subtle, dangerous deception.

The apostle Paul trained his son in the faith, Timothy, to preach the Word of God. Paul forewarned him, "The time is coming when people will not endure sound teaching, but having itching ears they will accumulate for themselves teachers to suit their own passions, and will turn away from listening to the truth and wander off into myths" (2 Timothy 4:3–4). We shouldn't be surprised that the same thing happens today.

LEAN BACK:

Have you listened to a source that made claims your itching ears wanted to hear, only to learn that those claims misuse God's Word or oppose it entirely? Have you followed a deceptive belief or mantra for a time? If so, what happened? How did you learn that you were deceived?

WHAT'S UP WITH THE BOOTSTRAPS?

Earlier, I mentioned the proverb "pulling ourselves up by our bootstraps." Did you realize this is both literally and figuratively a foolish venture? From the ground or from a seated position, try grabbing the straps of the boots on your feet or the laces on your shoes and standing. It physically cannot be done. You can only pull yourself up with the help of something solid or strong nearby like a chair, a grab bar, or the extended hand of another person. The expression originated in the nineteenth century, referring to a task that is impossible. "People understood the expression 'pulling yourself up by your bootstraps' to mean 'attempting to do something absurd' until roughly the 1920s, at which point it started to evolve toward the current understanding: to do something without any outside help. . . . The *idea* the expression is now meant to point to—that a lone individual can succeed through their own work, with no help from anyone else—is also fiction."[5]

We lack the self-power to pull ourselves up, so why might we be drawn to the deception of self-empowerment? Another soft sell—it sounds good: "Self-empowerment is the practice of intentionally choosing to be in control of your destiny," teaching the belief that you have the self-power to achieve your goals and take charge of your own life, that you have what it takes to overcome obstacles, and that you have everything you need within you.[6]

Self-empowerment movements include individualistic motivational mantras. For example, some mantras teach that if you lean in hard enough, press ahead, project enough confidence, and assert yourself, you'll accomplish your goals and dreams. While these behaviors have some merit (they promote a strong work ethic and an attitude of excellence, for instance), at some point they will fall short. Even from a worldly standpoint, "just trying harder," operating in the best self-strength we can muster, won't always cut the mustard! "Leaning in" cannot be about summoning our own strength. Rather, we rest in the One whose strength far surpasses our own: "Be strong in the Lord and in the strength of His might" (Ephesians 6:10).

LEAN BACK:

Do you know another expression that has come to mean something different than its original intent? Or an expression that makes sense but you don't know its origin? Examples to get you going: "nip it in the bud," "bite the bullet," "break the ice," and "don't throw the baby out with the bathwater."

WORLD:
Discover yourself.

JESUS:
Deny yourself.

WORLD: Follow your heart.

JESUS:
Follow Me.

WORLD: Believe in yourself.

JESUS:
Believe in Me.

WORLD:
Trust yourself.

JESUS:
Trust My Word.

Manifest?

I won't deny the culture's pull on me, encouraging me to take hold of my bootstraps! I've been fooled into thinking I can achieve my dreams if I just focus and plow forward! (I reason: surely God would want me to succeed if I'm doing this for His glory!) Social media posts and memes communicate that I can build myself up from within:

> *"Girl, manifestation is real. You can completely re-create yourself, create new habits, and live a life you're in love with. All that matters is that you decide today and never look back."*

> *"Be your own guru and trust yourself."*

> *"You are worthy enough to follow your dreams and manifest your desires."*

> *"If you believe you deserve it, the universe grants it."*

> *"Anything you desire is a preview of what is to come."*

LEAN BACK:

Share similar self-serving messages, memes, or quotes that you have seen. What makes them sound appealing? How may they be misleading?

Quotes like these go viral because, as followers reason, they appear too good not to share. But women have fallen prey to the charm of manifestation, a practice that has its roots in New Age philosophy and mysticism and that is connected to the popularity of vibes, energy channeling, and the like.[7]

According to an August 2022 *Breakpoint* article, "'Manifestation' is the practice of focused, intense thinking about what you want until you get it."[8] For instance, you might say something like, "I have the power to manifest my life in whatever way I want." A recent *Guardian* article stated, "Nearly every method asks that you act as though what you're attempting to manifest—love, money, a promotion or just a text back—is already true. . . . According to its practitioners, manifesting does not just prime you for success: it creates it."[9]

During a heart-to-heart conversation, my friend Sarah reminded me that self-empowerment messaging appears to work well when the outcome is one of success. But when failure or disappointment are the result, the same messaging is no longer helpful but actually self-defeating.

I understand the importance of setting goals, perhaps even creating a vision board to remind you what you're working toward and inspire you to work hard with laser-sharp focus. But "even the most imaginative and sincere visualization techniques cannot magically bend reality."[10] A practice like manifesting gives "the illusion of control. It assumes that internal focus can determine external realities."[11] Too often, I've visualized outcomes only to determine later that they were self-serving or didn't line up with God's lead for my life. He's in control, not me.

Rather than throw the proverbial baby out with the bathwater, let's consider what is worth keeping. I can look at goal setting in a godly light as I ask myself these questions: *Have I sought God's lead or my own? Is my goal God pleasing? What steps will I take, with God's help and a lot of prayer? Will I recognize that not meeting my goal may be a portion of what God has allowed in my life?*

P.S. Not all memes are meant to send us in the same wayward direction. I myself have posted a counterpoint: "The 'self-made' mindset is dangerous. You didn't get this far because of manifestation, 'good vibes,' or channeling energy. You're here because of a sovereign God faithful to fulfill His plans. You're not living in what you manifested; you're living in what God blessed you with." Amen.

MANIFEST!

The verb *manifest* means "to show or demonstrate plainly; reveal." Only our triune God can create something out of nothing, as He did in the beginning. Christ, who has been with the Father and the Spirit since before the beginning, revealed Himself as God in the flesh; He was made manifest among us. When Jesus performed His first miracle, John 2:11 tells us that He "manifested His glory."

> **LEAN IN #1:** In John 14:15–23, Jesus announced to His disciples the coming of the Helper, the Holy Spirit. What does Jesus mean by "manifest" in this passage?

> **LEAN IN #2:** How do Paul (in his letter to Timothy), Peter, and John all define manifest, by way of context, in these verses?
>
> *1 Timothy 3:16*
>
> *1 Peter 1:20–21*
>
> *1 John 1:1–3; 4:9*

"LEAN ON THE LORD, THE HOLY ONE OF ISRAEL"

What can we learn about leaning from the Israelites, God's chosen people? Too many times their wayward ways led God to discipline them out of love. Repeatedly, they fell prey to idolatry, foolishly leaning on false gods and forsaking the one true God. After His people failed to heed the prophets' repeated warnings, the Lord used enemy nations to remove them from Israel and send them into exile. The prophet Isaiah foretold these events. But even before Israel and Judah were sent into captivity, God promised that a remnant would return. Isaiah prophesied:

> **In that day the remnant of Israel and the survivors of the house of Jacob will no more lean on him who struck them, but will lean on the LORD, the Holy One of Israel, in truth. (Isaiah 10:20)**

Ahaz, king of Judah, leaned on the king of Assyria for support instead of looking to the Lord. His foolish decision would be the nation's demise. Assyria struck down Judah. (See 2 Kings 16:7–8 and 2 Chronicles 28:20–21.) Isaiah speaks of "that day" as the future day when God in His mercy would allow Israel to return from captivity. Isaiah prophesied there would be a day when God's people would no longer lean on powerful neighboring nations for support. Instead, they would lean on the Lord. They would not look to their oppressor—their false savior—but to God, their true Savior.

Isaiah's prophecy is doubly sweet because it's twofold; it refers not only to that future day but also to the day of Christ Jesus, when He returns!

"That day" would be one of victory from captivity; Israel would be restored to her homeland.

"That day" will be one of final victory from captivity to sin and death; all believers will receive complete restoration in Christ to our homeland of heaven.

(Isaiah and other prophets speak often of "that day" or "the day of the LORD," referring "to a time in which God dramatically reveals and/or executes His judgment by condemning the wicked and delivering the righteous. The prophets often use this phrase with reference to the end of history."[12] It is also referred to as "the Last Day, when the Lord returns to judge the ungodly and to redeem the faithful."[13])

Today, as then, God's people fall prey to idolatry of different kinds. We foolishly seek support from untrustworthy sources; we will suffer natural consequences when we lean in wayward, worldly ways. But Jesus has freed us from the captivity of our sin by His sacrifice in our place. We praise Him that we get to "lean on the LORD, the Holy One of Israel, in truth." By our Savior's strength, may we turn away from the false saviors from which we once sought support and see them for their deceptive claims and as the frauds that they are. The Lord welcomes us with open arms as we humbly return to Him, our Deliverer. We trust Him to preserve us in the one true faith, just as He preserved a remnant of His people Israel.

We come to Him shattered, struck down, or struggling . . . and we receive His restoring touch. Praise the God of Israel, the same Lord and Savior we worship today, for the first fulfillment and for the future and final fulfillment when Christ returns!

LEAN BACK:

On what "false saviors" have you leaned instead of the Lord? What did you hope they could deliver? Were you struck down? How did you recognize them as frauds?

When we've caved to the ways of the world or when we're distracted by its cares, we can ask ourselves the questions below. But our answers don't have the final say. We then come to Jesus, by the grace of God, and confess our wayward ways to Him.

As you address these questions, write out your honest answers, read the verses that follow, then receive a good word of grace. Read those paragraphs aloud, whether alone or with others, knowing they're true for you!

1. **WHAT AM I FIXING MY EYES ON**? That's where I find my focus, and I'm likely to follow this lead. Who or what is leading me? A self-help program? A social media influencer? A world leader? The divisions and disunity around me? Or am I fixing my focus on Jesus?

[Look] to Jesus, the founder and perfecter of our faith, who for the joy that was set before Him endured the cross, despising the shame, and is seated at the right hand of the throne of God. (Hebrews 12:2)

A GOOD WORD OF GRACE: Self-help has nothing on Him who founded my faith and is, even now, perfecting it, transforming me into His likeness (2 Corinthians 3:18). No other influencer can match the One who is seated at God's right hand. World leaders cannot compare with the One who reigns above all—the Savior of the world. Divisions and discord will one day give way to perfect unity because Jesus took all our sin and shame and nailed them to the cross.

2. **HOW AM I WALKING**? Are my choices worldly or godly? What does a watching world see in me? Whom do I aim to please, God or people?

Look carefully then how you walk, not as unwise but as wise, making the best use of the time, because the days are evil. (Ephesians 5:15–16)

Do not be conformed to this world, but be transformed by the renewal of your mind, that by testing you may discern what is the will of God, what is good and acceptable and perfect. (Romans 12:2)

For am I now seeking the approval of man, or of God? Or am I trying to please man? If I were still trying to please man, I would not be a servant of Christ. (Galatians 1:10)

A GOOD WORD OF GRACE: Praise the One who is the lamp to my feet and the light to my path (Psalm 119:105) so I can see where I'm going as He leads the way. When I stumble or wander with the unwise, He brings me back and even enables me to make the best use of the time I have.

Too often, I allow myself to be conformed to the ways of the world. I confess my conformity to the One who transforms me daily in Christ Jesus, renewing my mind and filling me with discernment, that I may know God's good and perfect will.

When I erroneously seek the approval of man, I read the inspired words of Paul, who sought to imitate Christ (1 Corinthians 11:1) as the Lord's servant, and I know that He who lives in me also forgives me. By His grace, I walk in love, a beloved child imitating God my Father (Ephesians 5:1–2).

3. WHICH WAY WILL I LEAN OR TURN?

Do not swerve to the right or to the left; turn your foot away from evil. (Proverbs 4:27)

And your ears shall hear a word behind you, saying, "This is the way, walk in it," when you turn to the right or when you turn to the left. (Isaiah 30:21)

A GOOD WORD OF GRACE: When I lean the wrong way, I'm bound to swerve into someone else, trip over myself, or fall flat on my face. Praise God for His forgiveness, accompanied by His strength, to pick me up, whisper directions in my ear, and send me on His way, that I may walk in it.

God's grace is sufficient to redirect my faulty focus, reestablish my wandering walk, and lead me to lean on Him. Fully forgiven, I rest my full weight upon the only One who is worthy! Amen.

LEANING-IN ACTION: Create an acrostic for LEAN or TRUST, based on something you studied today or a biblical concept you've learned. I'll give it a go:

Total

Rest

Under the

Savior's

Touch

Leaning on Jesus
WHEN WE DON'T
UNDERSTAND

Not Worthy of YOUR FULL WEIGHT

Imagine coming home at the end of an exhausting day. The sofa has never looked more appealing. Without hesitation, you put your full weight on it, confident of its purpose to hold you. To place complete confidence in something—to trust in it—is to lean on it. Conversely, what is NOT worthy of your full weight?

My friend Sarah found her middle school students leaning waaaay back in their classroom chairs, with only the back legs on the floor. She warned them that the chairs weren't designed to hold a person's weight on only two legs. But since several students had been leaning back in this manner for a while, they ignored her. Eventually—you guessed it—every chair wore down and broke. The students, one after another, fell off their chairs and onto the floor. They had put their full weight onto something that eventually gave way. When do we place false confidence in something that was not designed to hold up under our full weight, our complete trust?

Our own understanding is like the misused chair, tipped back on two legs. It is incapable of withstanding the burden of our weight; it was never meant to. When we ignore the voice of authority because we've been doing things our own way (and so far have succeeded), we foolishly lean on something that cannot hold us up over time. Eventually it will give way. The question is, how hard or far will we fall?

> **LEAN BACK:**
>
> Be careful what you're leaning back on! Admit it—you've leaned on something that gave way. What was it? Was anyone hurt? What did you learn from this incident?

When and why do you and I lean on Jesus? When we don't understand how He could save sinners like us. When we cannot understand a certain circumstance or how He could bring good out of suffering or struggle. When something in life makes little to no sense or seems impossible. When the Word of God tells us to.

TRUSTING AND LEANING

> Trust in the LORD with all your heart, and do not lean on your own understanding. (Proverbs 3:5)

When I look at this proverb, I often focus on the first phrase: "Trust in the LORD with all your heart." I reflect . . . and then worry: *Have I been trusting Him with all my heart? With all that I am?* The truth is I know I haven't, although I want to grow in trust.

My thoughts run amok, and my feelings betray me. I erroneously equate my difficult circumstances or pain with a lack of trust in God. I reason, *I wouldn't be struggling if I'd trusted God more.* We think we should "just try harder" to trust that He has everything under control, but in the moment, all we know is that we don't. We forget that, on our own, we lack trust no matter how hard we try. Praise God we're *not* on our own! He knows our thoughts, and He feels our pain. (He also knows how our feelings betray us.) He walks with us, allowing us to rest against Him as we struggle with our feelings and our fledgling trust. When we allow Him to work within us, our focus starts to shift from our circumstances to the cross. The pain may remain, at least for a time, as we endure our circumstances, but we know we're not alone in any circumstance. As Christ continuously draws us closer to Himself by the Gospel, the Holy Spirit strengthens our trust; it's His gift to us. We grow in faith, by the power of the Spirit. We desire to trust in the Lord with all our heart!

LEAN BACK: *can't do on our own!*

Do you realize that trust is a gift from God in Christ? Pause and thank God now for this amazing gift! Fully Rely on God (FROG) for salvation; you don't have to lean on your understanding, reason, or intellect. You cannot earn it and don't deserve it, but you are saved solely by God's grace through the gift of faith. Ask for increased trust as He helps you grow every day.

I would be wrong to conclude, as Andrew Steinmann puts it in his commentary on the Book of Proverbs, "that obtaining blessings from God is simply a matter of following instructions." The command to trust in the Lord is "ultimately . . . not [a] demand of the Law, but [an] invitation of the Gospel. . . . This is not mere human counsel, but divine guidance."[14]

Rest in Him, assured that even when your trust is lacking, He remains faithful. He invites you to trust in Him, and He guides you by the Spirit.

If you're like me, you haven't given as much thought to the second half of Proverbs 3:5. Only more recently have I paused to put greater emphasis on one little word: *lean*. Let's look at it more closely in the context of the entire verse.

Many of the proverbs penned by wise King Solomon contrast wisdom with foolishness. They often appear in contrasting couplet form, following a pattern of "the wise . . . , but the foolish . . . ." Proverbs 3:5 follows this pattern. The wise person is one who trusts in the Lord. (And not just a little, but with the whole heart!) The foolish one leans on—trusts in—his own understanding. Here, *trust* and *lean* have parallel meanings: to place complete trust in the Lord, the only One worthy of your full weight, is to lean on Him, even when you don't understand.

> *Lean (Hebrew: sha'an)[15] = to lean on, trust in, support; depicts an attitude of trust and ultimate dependence. The same Hebrew word is translated "rely" in Isaiah 50:10 and other places.*

> *Trust (Hebrew: batach)[16] = to trust, to trust in, have confidence in. The same Hebrew word is used in Isaiah 50:10 and in many psalms and proverbs.*

LEAN IN #1: Read Isaiah 50:10 and focus on the words that parallel one another. Remember that "rely" in this verse is the same Hebrew word for "lean" in Proverbs 3:5. Isaiah is God's servant, calling people to obey his voice because he speaks for God. What will happen for the person who relies on God?

I lean *not* on my own understanding. Proverbs 28:26 is even more to the point: "Whoever trusts in his own mind is a fool." According to Steinmann, this could also be translated as "one who trusts in his (own) heart—*he is the one who is* a fool. . . . Such

you never fail if you keep trying.

LEANING-IN ACTION: What wandering, worrisome thoughts would you like to take captive? (See 2 Corinthians 10:5b.) Take them to God in prayer, and weigh them against His Word.

a person contradicts the counsel in [Proverbs] 3:5 to 'trust in Yahweh with all your heart.' He is an unbeliever."[17] So what do I do, with the Lord's help? I lean into His full knowledge, complete understanding, and perfect wisdom.

LEAN BACK:

Even when I don't see His work, feel His presence, or understand what's going on, I can trust that He *is* working. I believe that He will use (insert any circumstance) for good as He works in and through me for His purpose.

:26 works together with the Holy Spirit

LEAN IN #2: Write the comforting words of Romans 8:28:

All that happens to us is working for our good if we love God and fit into His plans.

Meditate on this verse. You are a chosen child of God, called according to His purpose. What does this verse say that you know? Courageously consider what "things" you can trust God to work together for good, even if you can't comprehend how it could be possible.

He may use our struggles on our journey as preparation for yet another purpose to which He is calling us. You see, the God who created and shaped us for His purpose knows every part of our journey from His eternal perspective of completion. We cannot rest on our own lack of understanding; rather, we lean into God's strong arms on every dark day and in the midst of every circumstance. We surrender our situations to Him and receive rest.

Puzzling

Since God's ways and thoughts are higher than mine (Isaiah 55:8–9), it's no wonder I don't always understand how He is working or what He is doing or for what purpose. I trust that He knows.

"For now we see in a mirror dimly [reflection], but then face to face. Now I know in part; then I shall know fully, even as I have been fully known" (1 Corinthians 13:12). The Greek word to describe what we see "in a mirror dimly" (or "reflection" in some translations) is *ainigma*—a riddle, an enigma, obscure.[18] What we see is puzzling; it's difficult to fully understand.

After every difficult situation, I want to be able to say, "Ah-ha! I get it now!" I would love to receive answers to my "whys" and "hows" and "how longs." But the answers may elude me; they may not be found in the partial understanding available to me today. When Christ returns, though, I will receive perfect perspective and every puzzling riddle will be answered. Meanwhile, it's comforting to remember that my Creator knows me fully. In fact, He has infinite knowledge, understanding, and insight over all things. He sees completion when I only see the messy middle, and He does all things for His greater purpose. So I lay my lack of understanding at His feet, and I trust that one day I will see fully what I only see in small part for now. I focus on His promise—that He works all things together for larger-than-life-size *good*. My friend Darcy Paape sent me these welcome words in the middle of this messy manuscript-in-progress: "Just a reminder that it is okay to be messy because that is why we NEED Jesus. He shows up in our messy story as the Messiah."

I trust that God has a purpose for every detail of my life. He works deftly with those details and weaves them together with other people's details too, creating an enormous tapestry that will, upon its completion, reveal His reasons in all their beauty and intricacy. Remembering His care over every detail, I place myself complete with my lack of understanding—in His hands.

LEANING-IN ACTION: Put together a puzzle, but don't look at the box. As you work, remember that God sees the completed picture of your life and knows when each piece will come together. Look at a single piece. Does it give you a glimpse of the big picture? Relate this to your life in Christ.

SEEK UNDERSTANDING. WAIT. WHAT?

Although the Lord commands us not to lean on our own understanding, He is not telling us to check our intellect at the door. It's not as though our understanding and faith are mutually exclusive. In fact, the opposite is true! In several other proverbs (and many other places in Scripture), the Lord exhorts us to *seek* understanding.

LEAN IN #1: Look up Proverbs 2:2; 3:13; 5:1; 19:8; and 23:23. What words in each verse make it clear that we are to seek understanding? *Good judgement, common sense, wisdom, listen, watch yourself, get the facts*

Clearly, we should desire wisdom and understanding, so what's different about the understanding mentioned in Proverbs 3:5, and why are we *not* to lean on it? We are not to lean on our *own* understanding. In other words, we're not to trust in our assumptions or conclusions drawn from our limited view or perspective. Our own understanding is simply incapable of bearing our full weight!

> Be not wise in your own eyes; fear the LORD, and turn away from evil. It will be healing to your flesh and refreshment to your bones. (Proverbs 3:7–8)

As we live out our faith, by God's grace, we seek His wisdom and His understanding over our own. Wisdom from the Word rules over our reasoning. Only His Word has supreme authority, determining right from wrong, good from evil, wise from foolish. We are resting our intellect upon the intellect of God. What could be wiser?!

So many of our struggles and conflicts, the sources of so much anxiety and fear, are a result of leaning on our own understanding. Regularly, we could cite secular sources championing worldly wisdom and even claiming that those who trust in the Lord are irrational or ignorant. But worldly understanding, apart from the wisdom of the Lord, changes like the wind. It's subjective and limited, and often mistaken or convoluted. We could act impulsively according to what we perceive or feel in the moment, or we could trust the objective truth provided by a perfectly reliable source. Why would we trust such woefully limited understanding when we have access to God's complete, limitless understanding?

Let the Lord lead you, and trust Him to help: "Commit your way to the Lord; trust in Him, and He will act" (Psalm 37:5).

We live in a culture that frequently says, "I just don't understand," and since we've come to expect instant answers from myriad sources, we reason we should dismiss something beyond our comprehension. Yet God is a mystery, and although our understanding is limited, we receive, by faith "all the riches of full assurance of understanding and the knowledge of God's mystery, which is Christ, in whom are hidden all the treasures of wisdom and knowledge" (Colossians 2:2–3).

LEAN IN #2: Read 1 Corinthians 2:6–16. How could this passage help you address your own doubts or those of others when you are tempted to dismiss something of God because you just don't understand? How are you able to understand the truth of God? Who is "the natural person" and why doesn't he understand? What do you think it means to have "the mind of Christ"? *being in the Word* *sinful self*

"No wisdom, no understanding, no counsel can avail against the Lord" (Proverbs 21:30). In Steinmann's words, "Human wisdom can succeed only if it is aligned with, and derived from, God's own wisdom. This is a warning for believers not to trust their own understanding . . . because of the sin that still clings to all people in this life, even the spiritually wise. . . It is important to compare our thoughts and desires to God's will as revealed in His Word to ensure that they are not skewed by our sinful inclinations."[19] *Discernment*

LEAN BACK:

Examine your heart's desires, your inward thoughts. Take them to God's Word and compare them there. Pause to pray for His wisdom and discernment as you remember His authority and grace over you.

LEAN IN #3: Read the verses in the first column that correspond with the attribute of God in the second column. Some will affirm the reasons we trust in the Lord; others will remind us why we don't lean on our own understanding. Fill in what you learn from these verses:

Scripture	Trust in the Lord	Do not lean on your own understanding
Proverbs 14:12	God does not lie.	
Jeremiah 17:9	Only the Lord knows	the heart is the most deceitful thing
Hebrews 6:18	God doesn't lie God promised	we can count on His promise and oath
Numbers 23:19	God does not change.	
Malachi 3:6	God's mercy endures forever	Trust in the Lord
James 1:17	He shines forever without change or shadow	whatever is good & perfect comes from God.
Psalm 147:5	God understands and knows all things	
1 Corinthians 13:12	God sees into my heart	some day see God in His completeness
1 John 3:20	He knows every thing we do	bad conscience or did something wrong

Paired perfectly with Proverbs 3:5 is the verse that follows it: "In all your ways acknowledge Him, and He will make straight your paths" (v. 6). From our hearts and minds to our hands and feet, we trust and acknowledge the Lord to lead our lives. All our heart → all our ways! God's promise to direct our paths is rich in imagery because "paths in ancient Israel were often winding, tortuous roads that took much effort on the part of travelers. A straight path, which would be relatively easy to traverse, was rare. . . . The ability to walk on this path is a gift from God, received through faith, that is, simple trust in God. . . . The metaphor of the path is . . . [an] invitation of the Gospel to repentance, faith, and trust."[20]

God isn't asking you to figure it out.

He's asking you to trust that He already has.

LEAN BACK:

Imagine a clear path. Maybe it's shaded by a canopy of trees, but light shines through. Your direction is clear, but it doesn't look easy. It's a rough road, and a bit bumpy along the way. But by His grace and with direction from His Word, God is guiding you to His promised destination. He will get you there!

Yes, we will face struggles and strife, but we have these promises to guide us. He gives us His Word that we can trust Him . . . with all our heart. We acknowledge Him . . . in all our ways. He directs our paths. Amen.

Cliché

"Don't worry; everything is going to be okay."

"God has a plan, just you wait and see!"

"Just trust; God's got this!"

Life is messy and our understanding is limited. So is our perspective and wisdom. When a friend or loved one hurts, there is a time to speak and a time to just "be" beside them. Sometimes words don't aid in understanding because only God can make sense of the situation. Lean on Him in your own lack of understanding and as you ask Him to direct your words, responses, and gestures toward those you sit beside in love.

When we suddenly lost my dear cousin Bruce, I mourned alongside our family and especially with his widow, Wendy. We cried together. "It's not fair. It's awful. It doesn't make sense. Why would God allow this?" Our words expressed our lack of understanding. Wendy is a precious woman of faith. She trusts God amid her suffering. And although I wanted to, I couldn't come up with anything that would take the pain away. So often, our own failure to understand has us grasping at straws, seeking a quick answer as a soothing balm. But trying to tidy up messy feelings or mend broken hearts with fix-it words seldom works. Yet we can simply speak truth in the most tender way. Wendy could share that she knows her beloved husband is with Jesus. She has eternal hope in her Savior. And yes, knowing these truths makes a difference. We grieve, but we grieve with hope. We pray for and with one another. We wrestle with questions, even as we rest in the final answer: certain hope of Bruce's salvation—and ours—in Jesus.

LEAN BACK:

Have you been at a loss for words as you attempt to comfort a loved one or as you face your own pain? Rest next to one another as you lean on Jesus together. Trust Him to give you words when they're needed, based on the hope you have in Him. Speak truth tenderly. It's okay to rest in silence too. Your presence speaks for itself.

JESUS WEPT

When Jesus arrived in Bethany following Lazarus's death, He mourned with Mary and Martha in the loss of their brother. Jesus drew near to their grief. He wept with them, even though He knew He was about to raise His dear friend from his tomb. Jesus knows our pain too. He draws near. He weeps with us and walks with us in our grief. Although He can—and will—tidy every mess perfectly upon His return, in our times of grief, Jesus leans in. He welcomes His followers to lean on Him in our sorrow. He will provide comfort as only He can.

> **LEAN IN #1:** Read John 11:32–44. Place yourself near Bethany, watching as Mary approaches Jesus and falls at His feet. See the Jews weeping and note their response as they see Jesus weeping too. What feelings are expressed in this passage, including those of Jesus? Watch as Jesus prays in the presence of the mourners. Share additional thoughts as you meditate on this passage.

Trusting the Lord to lead me with wisdom in His Word, I pray that I may bring His hope and comfort to others as they mourn, that I may weep with those who weep (Romans 12:15) while trusting in the resurrection as Martha did (John 11:27). We may grapple with what we cannot understand, but He is teaching us to trust that He does.

"WHY ME, GOD?"

We've all had those tough times in life when we've taken some unexpected hits or a circumstance has sent us reeling. When our head stops spinning, maybe the only words we can muster are "Why me?!"

Ask the Savior to give [you] eyes to see beyond [your] circumstances and courage to say, 'Why not me? He loves me enough to guide me through anything this messed up world tries to throw at me. He loves me enough to allow these struggles so that I may see my need for my Savior and learn to rest in His strength (not my own), even as He

Here is to
not knowing.

Here is to
praying honestly.

Here is to leaning
in and listening.

Here is to trusting.

"God,

I don't know.

Amen."[55]

—Tanner Olson

may use these struggles to sharpen my character and give me growth in Him.' In this world, [you] will have troubles [John 16:33], but the soothing balm of His grace is much greater than the worst . . . pain. He overcame sin, death, and the devil at the cross for [you], His chosen child.[21]

LEAN IN #2: Why might God allow struggles, including those you just don't understand? Which of the possibilities mentioned below gives you reassurance or peace? Talk or write about it. Share other possibilities you have that are not mentioned here.

To see your need for your Savior

To learn to rest in His strength

To sharpen your character

To give you growth in Him

The "whys" of the psalmists often comfort me because I cry them too. King David and other writers wrestled with a lack of answers: "O my God, I cry by day, but You do not answer, and by night, but I find no rest" (Psalm 22:2). "Hear, O LORD, when I cry aloud; be gracious to me and answer me!" (Psalm 27:7). They laid their laments before the Lord, trusting that He heard their cries, even when He didn't respond with a recognizable answer. Right now, there are so many things I don't get. *Why did my little sister suffer from a seizure disorder? Why do some people endure more difficulties than others? Why don't I receive relief from some bad habits when I've been praying about them for so long?* This side of eternity, I may not receive recognizable answers to countless "whys." Yet I trust God. He knows all. He is the refuge and the rock on whom I lean.

> Trust in Him at all times, O people; pour out your hearts before Him; God is a refuge for us. (Psalm 62:8)

Because of my "whys," I am more understanding of others who

LEANING-IN ACTION: The adage "lay your cares at His feet" illustrates our need to bring every concern to the Lord. Make this tangible: write your cares on a sticky note and place it beneath a cross on the wall to remind you that you're taking it to the Lord and leaving it there.

wrestle with their own unanswered questions, even if their situations are radically different from mine.

When I'm wrestling with "why," I tend to lean harder on Jesus. With His help, I shift my focus to "who"—to the One who holds me, unanswered questions and all.

LEAN BACK:

What "whys" do you wrestle with? Write them down and take them to the Lord. Lean back as you pour out your heart to Him, leave your unanswered questions with Him, and trust Him to exchange them for His peace. He holds you, and He knows what you need.

"I Believe! HELP MY UNBELIEF!"

My faith feels shallow in those moments when I realize I've stopped praying for something because the situation is outside my control. I've incorrectly concluded that God is going to do with it what He will and nothing I pray will make a difference. But I know better. With His help, I recall:

- ❤ His faithfulness in the past.

- ❤ His command to pray.

- ❤ His ability to work things out and answer my prayers amid my shallow faith and doubt.

LEAN IN #1: Read Mark 9:17–27. Pay attention to the father who approaches Jesus. After explaining his situation, what does he ask, and what's significant about how he asks? Write Jesus' response in verse 23: *Cast out the deamon Father confessed he had faith Anything is possible if you have faith*

What do you make of the father's exclamation in verse 24? How could this encounter apply to us today? *Wanted to have more faith.*

Maybe the father had concluded that his son couldn't be healed. With just a flicker of faith, however, he came to Jesus. Maybe he had heard of Jesus' miracles. Without a doubt, the father's faith grew considerably that day.

God's ability to heal, solve, or remedy a situation is far greater than the situation itself. When He doesn't choose the method, direction, or timing we envision or prefer, we may not recognize His answer. The father received a direct and recognizable answer to his prayer, but God in His wisdom may answer our prayers in ways that differ from our desires. That does not make Him any less caring, capable, or compassionate. In this father's fledgling faith, he was embraced by Jesus, and we can trust that we are too! A friend of mine told me, "I'm confident that Jesus is at work in my situation, even when I don't see or feel it. I trust it will glorify God, but maybe not in my preferred way." By His grace, we can choose to trust Him to provide the best answer and the right decision, no matter what the outcome looks like to us. We rest in His care; He desires our best.

OBEDIENCE, EVEN WHEN WE DON'T UNDERSTAND

LEAN BACK:

When has God answered a prayer in a way that was, at first, unrecognizable to you? What led you to recognize it later? Maybe you're still wrestling with what appears to be unanswered prayer. What will help you rest in His care, regardless of the eventual outcome?

Sometimes, trust doesn't seem so difficult. Other times, our faith and obedience are tested when we cannot see how or where God is working. How do we persevere when we don't see evidence of impact? We keep His promises before us and remember His words: "Now faith is the assurance of things hoped for, the conviction of things not seen" (Hebrews 11:1).

Resolution or results don't necessarily come because you force them but because the Lord chooses to use you in your imperfect obedience that you humbly offer to Him even when something doesn't make sense or fit with your plans.

As I was penning the words that now fill these pages, it seemed to me that obedience to this task would look like having my nose in my notes and my fingers on my laptop whenever possible. When interpersonal opportunities came at me repeatedly, I was compelled to say yes to them on a number of days when I'd previously scheduled seclusion. I questioned every yes, thinking I was confusing these interruptions with procrastination. Both priorities tugged at me until one morning when my son Chris was driving me to the airport. I'd lamented to him during our drive, and as we neared the terminal, he gave me a thoughtful, wise reply. Chris reassured me that my obedience included interactions with others that served to bless them, refuel me, and even provide a portion of what God would use in my writing. Touché, Chris, touché!

I STILL PRAISE YOU!

The Lord is sovereign over every situation. Isn't that relieving news? We can rest in Him when our circumstances would otherwise have us restless, hopeless, or anxious. Right in the middle of

> ## LEAN BACK:
> In what ways is God using you today, as you humbly offer your imperfect obedience to Him? Remember that He perfects you in Christ and chooses to use you for His purpose; He may even lead you to something different from what you had planned.

our lack of understanding, we can praise Him because we know He has our situation—and us—in His capable hands. The peace He extends is truly beyond our understanding (Philippians 4:7), but we receive it by His grace. With Isaiah, we can say, "You keep [her] in perfect peace whose mind is stayed on You, because [she] trusts in You" (Isaiah 26:3). Even if we don't feel His peace, we can trust that this precious fruit of the Spirit (Galatians 5:22) is ours by faith, deeper than our feelings.

While we praise Him, He is working. He leads us:

- from restlessness toward rest in Him,

- from hopelessness to His assurance of hope, and

- from anxiety to the promise of His peace.

What if our struggles continue to plague us, even amid our praise? God is not surprised by our fears or feelings. He uses them to have us lean even harder, to rest in His arms as we proclaim to the world that the Lord is worthy of all our praise! (See Psalm 18:3.)

In Psalm 40:4, King David declares, "Blessed is the man who makes the LORD his trust." I want this kind of trust, don't you? And

LEANING-IN ACTION: Wherever you go today, watch for a single word to stand out to you: on a billboard, at a store, on a screen, or the like. Write it down and relate it to your trust in God. Be creative; make a connection!

it's ours in Christ! Let's turn to the verses immediately preceding this one for confirmation of lessons we're learning along the way:

> I waited patiently for the LORD; He inclined to me and heard my cry. He drew me up from the pit of destruction, out of the miry bog, and set my feet upon a rock, making my steps secure. He put a new song in my mouth, a song of praise to our God. (Psalm 40:1–3a)

LEAN IN #2: David admits he is blessed; he has made the Lord his trust (Psalm 40:4). Where had he found himself and what did he do? What did the Lord do for him? What does this say to you about trials? Where is God in them? Taking cues from King David, how can you respond to the Lord's help? *many blessings are given those who trust in the Lord.*

Trust is often formed or fortified in the muck and the mire of life. *Wait, do I still want this kind of trust?* To be clear, God doesn't desire us to endure pits of destruction or miry bogs just to make us stronger. He may, however, allow something in our lives that will provide opportunities for our growth. The muck and the mire exist because we live in a fallen world. In it, we may more readily see our need for Him.

The Lord may be working in a way I cannot understand, especially when that way is difficult. I may have to wait during a challenging season while I cry to Him in prayer. I may sit in the pit of destruction or wade through a miry bog for a while, but I am confident, as David was, that God will incline to me. He will hear my cry, draw me up, and set my feet on a rock. He will send me forward, secure in my steps. I will sing the praise He puts in my mouth! And He will even use my witness: "Many will see and fear, and put their trust in the LORD" (Psalm 40:3b).

Jesus is the Rock

LEAN IN #3: Read Isaiah 26:4. How do Isaiah's words relate with the resolve of Psalm 40:1–4? *Trust in the Lord God always, He is your everlasting strength. many blessings are given to those who trust in the Lord.*

Rev. Dr. Dale Meyer said this of our struggles:

> The earthly situation that stresses you is also a spiritual opportunity to be strengthened by the Spirit in the life of faith, of trusting God's promises. None of us seeks out

adversity but it comes. You have to believe that God has protected us from more troubles than we can know, but He doesn't ward off all our problems. Like a loving parent, His hand reaches to lead us through the long days we have to endure. "Now for a little while, if necessary, you have been grieved by various trials, so that the tested genuineness of your faith—more precious than gold that perishes though it is tested by fire—may be found to result in praise and glory and honor at the revelation of Jesus Christ" (1 Peter 1:6–7).[22]

May there be a new song in your mouth today too! A song of praise and glory and honor to our God as you look forward to the day of Christ Jesus.

Facing an UNKNOWN FUTURE

If our past was wrought with pain, sometimes we are hesitant to embrace the present because we're peering in the rearview mirror. Or perhaps we are looking forward, but we are wondering when we will drive over the next set of spike strips! We may be hesitant to look to the future for fear of detours, closed roads, or fender benders.

We know we can trust God's promises, but our experiences may have diverted our attention; our circumstances have made us skeptical that our future can be filled with good things. Maybe we have convinced ourselves that pain is punishment for our lack of faith or having not enough trust. But that's not the way of our Lord! While we may face earthly consequences for our sins, we have a Savior who faced full and final punishment for them on our behalf at the cross.

Christ's faithfulness is not contingent upon the strength of our faith. "If we are faithless, He remains faithful" (2 Timothy 2:13). With the help of the Holy Spirit, we can release the doubt or hesitancy we cling to. With open arms, we embrace His trustworthy promises.

Can we see beyond our past experience to the possibilities that lie ahead?

Can we recognize the painful parts as stepping stones—preparation and opportunities—for growth?

Perhaps our past has shaped us for today's challenges and a future known only to God. May we see His hands at work, in painful *and* joyful times, knowing He walks with us through both.

As we peer forward into the unknown, what do we know? What promises can we cling to?

God goes before us.

Nothing is unknown to Him.

There is not one thing He doesn't understand.

He will work on our behalf.

No matter what comes, God will be true to His Word.

We can lean on His unchanging promises amid every changing circumstance. When we face the *un*known today and the *uncer*tainty of tomorrow, we *know* He is faithful; we are *certain* of His promises for us in Christ.

> **LEAN BACK:**
> Pray some of God's promises today, resting in the truth that "all the promises of God find their Yes in [Christ]" (2 Corinthians 1:20). A couple places to start: "It is the LORD who goes before you. He will be with you; He will not leave you or forsake you. Do not fear or be dismayed" (Deuteronomy 31:8). "O LORD, You have searched me and known me! You know when I sit down and when I rise up; You discern my thoughts from afar" (Psalm 139:1–2). Refer to promises shared earlier in this chapter too.

PEACE THAT SURPASSES UNDERSTANDING

Kip and Deb's family began the most difficult trial of their lives nearly eleven years ago. Their then twelve-year-old son, Kyle, was diagnosed with osteosarcoma—bone cancer in his femur.

In the next six years, Kyle underwent scores of treatments and major surgeries; he endured mouth sores, hair loss, nausea, crutches, and therapy. Deb spoke to me of the peace they possessed, even in the darkest moments of those days, and it was not something she shared lightly or tritely. She knew this must be peace from the Lord, the "peace of God, which surpasses all understanding" (Philippians 4:7), as they faced seemingly insurmountable trials. One ineffective treatment followed another. Statistics were not in Kyle's favor. Eventually, treatment options were exhausted. Following the final chemo treatment, which looked unproductive, the cancer was . . . gone. Against all odds!

This family persevered in Christ's strength, acknowledging that they leaned on Him every day. What a witness they were!

They touched hospital staff, sports figures, friends, classmates, and complete strangers with the love of Christ. Amid their trial, Deb shared, "God gives us our kids for such a short time. Kyle is mine, but he really isn't; he belongs to the Lord. And our lives here are so short compared to eternity. Our trial was made easier when we compared it to an eternity with Jesus free of fear, trials, and pain."[23]

Today, this family's hope is sure and certain; their peace is profound! Now five years cancer-free, Kyle continues to be a walking miracle, steel femur and all! Last fall, Kip said, "Ten years ago today was the worst day of our lives as Kyle was diagnosed with Osteosarcoma. Now, after years of chemo, several clinical trials, twelve surgeries, and four relapses, he is living his best life! Praise be to God, to whom we owe all thanks!"[24]

> **LEAN IN #1:** Familiarize yourself with Philippians 4:6–7 and meditate over these verses now. Contrast what you should be anxious about with what you can pray about. With what attitude will you bring your requests to the Lord? What kind of trade does God make on your behalf, and why does it surpass all understanding? What does this mean?

Won't worry about anything – pray about everything. Prayer will keep your heart quiet. Thank Him for His answers.

OUR BUCKLER

Our understanding is limited, at best, and flawed, for sure. It will buckle or break when tested. Tainted by sin and left to our own devices, we could easily lean in a self-serving direction. God's ways may be difficult to understand, even contrary to our desires, but Scripture shows us again and again that His ways are best. Not only will He never fail us, but because He is our Rock, we can rest our entire weight upon Him and He won't be moved. "His faithfulness is a shield and buckler" (Psalm 91:4). Should we buckle, He catches us in His everlasting arms: "The eternal God is your dwelling place, and underneath are the everlasting arms" (Deuteronomy 33:27). This verse was the inspiration behind this hymn, published in 1887. Lean in and listen:

Leaning on the Everlasting Arms

What a fellowship, what a joy divine,
Leaning on the everlasting arms;
What a blessedness, what a peace is mine,
Leaning on the everlasting arms.
Refrain:
Leaning, leaning,
Safe and secure from all alarms;
Leaning, leaning,
Leaning on the everlasting arms.

Oh, how sweet to walk in this pilgrim way,
Leaning on the everlasting arms;
Oh, how bright the path grows from day to day,
Leaning on the everlasting arms. *Refrain*

What have I to dread, what have I to fear,
Leaning on the everlasting arms?
I have blessed peace with my Lord so near,
Leaning on the everlasting arms. *Refrain*
—Elisha A. Hoffman

LEAN IN #2: According to this inspirational hymn's verses and refrain, what do we receive as we lean on the Lord's everlasting arms? Where might you make a connection with Proverbs 3:6? *In every thing you do, put God first... He will direct you.*

PUT YOUR FULL WEIGHT INTO IT!

I overanalyze decisions, agonize over details, and wonder if I'm on the right path. While I'm contemplating a decision, people may even ask, "Which way are you leaning?" That makes me think of helping my husband fix our wooden fence that was leaning from the force of last winter's wind. Although I pushed hard against it,

"Eagles Wings"

LEANING-IN ACTION: Name a favorite hymn, praise song, or other song. Lean in and listen closely to the message. What's your take-away? How may it help you when you're struggling to understand something?

I was struggling to straighten it enough for him to put props in place. He hollered, "Put your full weight into it!" So I planted my feet and leaned forward with my full weight, hoping it wouldn't sway forward so far that I would fall flat on my face. We managed to fix the fence.

I make decisions harder than they have to be. I'm afraid I may sway in the wrong direction and fall flat. So I look to the wisdom of Proverbs 3:5–6 as a reminder to trust in the Lord, lean my full weight upon Him, and be confident that He will make my path straight. I look at my choices and ponder every option, wondering which He will reveal with flashing-light clarity. But what if both (or more) options are good and God-pleasing? If they each pass the litmus test of His Word, maybe I'm free to make either choice. Instead of obsessing over options, thinking I will somehow lose His blessing if I choose the wrong one, I can choose confidently as I continue to seek His lead and acknowledge Him as Lord of my days and decisions. I can put my full weight into each decision.

When you and I know God for who He is and all He has done—the One who is our Creator, Savior, Counselor—we can be confident that He who knows all things will work them together for good. To know Him is to trust Him. I can trust that God will work through each choice I make and continue to walk beside me, straightening and illuminating the path ahead. In every decision, God is with me, loving me, and leading me.

LEAN BACK:

Go outside and look at the horizon, if you can. There's a lot happening out there, beyond the horizon, that you simply cannot see. Thank God for the limitation of vision that permits us to see only what's within our view. May we spend our lifetime learning and seeking God's desires for us as we walk by faith and not by sight (2 Corinthians 5:7), trusting Him for the future beyond our current horizon.

Leaning on Jesus
WHEN WE'RE
WEARY

Rest FOR THE WEARY

I guilted myself for feeling weary. I knew that others had much greater reasons for feeling this way. One dear friend was wrapping up a tough year of nursing school while suffering the sudden loss of her mama. Other friends also had a strenuous school year as educators; they faced new challenges with students who were struggling personally and academically. Still other friends in medical professions were worn out due to staff shortages and long shifts with no changes in sight.

Weariness hits all of us for assorted reasons and in various seasons. I realized that my causes of spiritual fatigue didn't need to be catastrophic. Nor did I need to compare them to the fatigue of others for validation. I knew only that I was weary. Weary of caving to temptation, feeding my unhealthy habits that had developed or worsened during the pandemic. I was weary of the never-ending flow of information, reminding me of division in our nation and violence around the world. Weary of writing deadlines and travel preparations. Weary of my own brokenness. My husband needed a rejuvenating break from the kinds of ministry demands that perhaps only pastors and church workers understand. We both knew we needed to retreat for physical rest and soul care.

Blessed by the generosity of others, our family received a ten-day respite to Hawaii. I tucked a new journal in my bag, and, aboard a turbulent flight, I wrote,

> **LEAN BACK:**
> What has made you weary in this season? Or for what reason(s) have you been weary?

As we fly to Hawaii, I anticipate REST. Cory needs real rest from the rigors of ministry. We're taking precious time away . . . and I pray we will embrace the kind of rest that includes (1) savoring the shared adventures and time with each other and with our kids; (2) recognizing God's hand in our days, interactions, and memorable moments; (3) taking in His wondrous creation that's unlike most of our everyday world; (4) seeking His lead to give us rest—physical, mental, and spiritual rest—as we receive (and generously give) the grace that we so need. May I sit at His feet throughout our vacay and let Him give me rest. Real rest.

For I will satisfy the weary soul, and every languishing soul I will replenish. (Jeremiah 31:25)

Deliberately seeking rest en route, recognizing that it could not be found apart from the Lord, and even journaling about it with anticipation, I found myself more intentional throughout our vacation. And the Holy Spirit continued to nudge me toward daily quiet time in the Word and in my journaling space.

After we returned home, I revisited a *Portals of Prayer* devotion that I'd read only a week before we'd departed for Hawaii:

Jesus understands weariness. He faced extreme temptations of hunger and thirst in the wilderness all alone. Besieged by noisy crowds demanding answers and miracles, Jesus would retreat to rest and pray. With a heavy burden of our sins pressed upon His shoulders, Jesus prayed, tired but determined. Spat upon, whipped, and humiliated for things He hadn't done, He knows how weary life can be. Our Savior knows the battle for our peace is won. Exhausted, He paid the price for our redemption.[25]

LEANING-IN ACTION: Pick or purchase a fresh flower. Lean in, inhale, and capture the scent. Does it evoke a memory? Does it help you to simply take a breath, a reminder to rest?

Yes, Jesus understands weariness. When I battle temptation, I know He fought it too. When I am worn down by daily demands, I remember He faced them as well. Even the Son of God sought rest with the Father. Again, let me say Jesus understands. He has been there. He bore the full weight of our sins on His shoulders, and He won the victory for you and me. He gives us perfect peace, eternal rest, and renewed strength for the weariness we face today.

LEAN BACK:

Picture time away from your routine that allows you real rest. Write specific opportunities after each idea below. You don't need to wait for vacation to intentionally seek rest.

1. **SAVOR A SHARED MOMENT WITH LOVED ONES, FULLY PRESENT**. Avoid distractions.

2. **RECOGNIZE GOD'S HAND IN YOUR DAY**. Where is He working? What memory are you making in your interactions with another person?

3. **VIEW THE WONDER OF GOD'S CREATION, EVEN IF YOUR VIEW IS FAMILIAR**. What do you notice? Praise Him for it!

4. **TRUST YOUR SAVIOR TO PROVIDE REAL REST THROUGH HIS FORGIVENESS, WON FOR YOU AT THE CROSS**. Sit at His feet in His Word.

LEAN IN #1: Earlier, I spoke of Christ's gifts to us in the victory He won at the cross: the perfect peace, eternal rest, and renewed strength for the weariness we face today. Read what Scripture says about these gifts:

John 14:27—What's unique about the peace we receive in Christ?

Revelation 14:13—In John's vision of heaven, who receives eternal rest?

1 Peter 5:10—How will our strength be restored when we're depleted and weary?

REST FOR THE WEARY, REVISITED

Multitudes of people were weary when they came out of COVID confinement, recovering from illness, contending with restrictions, and experiencing uncertainty. All around me, I heard sentiments that included a longing to return to some semblance of normalcy that had been missing for so long. That's why we've seen a frenzy of movement to the places and events we had missed. Some have scurried back to the workplace and the routine of the nine-to-five. Many have traveled to vacation destinations or flocked to restaurants, movie theaters, and more. Why? To feed a yearning for all to be well again, to refuel from the depletion that the COVID crisis and other circumstances have caused. However, the overwhelming result is that the rest we chased does not satisfy us in the ways we expected. Again, we are reminded that mere activity cannot provide what our hungry, weary souls crave. My friend Sarah remarked, "We're striving to return to a pre-COVID world, yet we have post-COVID needs, physically, emotionally, and most significantly, spiritually. We are living in a time of soul-weary people who are exhausted, worn-down, and charged to pop off at any disappointment, let-down, or disagreement."

Depleted and deprived, we hunger for nourishment, but we won't find true satisfaction via long walks on a beach or hikes in the woods, aboard a cruise or beneath a beautiful sunset. It *can* be found in the One who created every breathtaking view as we let God fill us, as we turn to Him for renewal, restoration, and respite. May we long for more of Him, not mere normalcy. May we stop settling for rest in fleeting moments and find genuine rest in His timeless Word. *and sacraments.*

Reflecting on my Hawaiian vacation, I was reminded just how much I need daily rest with Jesus, whether I'm on vacation or at home. Whether I lie on a beach or sit in my backyard, or whether I rest under Hawaii's palm trees or Nebraska's aspens.

I don't have to wait for someone to give me permission to rest.

I don't have to prove that my weariness is great enough to be worthy of rest. I don't have to wait for another person's invitation to rest either. Jesus invites me every day. He knows I need it. May I be so drawn to the help Jesus provides that I lean in—that I trust Him with all my heart, resting the full weight of my burdens, my day, and myself on Him.

JESUS NEEDED REST

What examples did Jesus give us when He was weary from His workload of ministering to the masses, healing the sick, traveling to teach, and more?

> **LEAN IN #2:** Learn more about Jesus' rest in Matthew 14:23; Mark 1:35; Mark 6:31–32; Luke 6:12. What was His priority when He rested? Where did He go? And how did He encourage His disciples?

Jesus went away by Himself for time alone with the Father. He woke early and began His day in prayer. He retreated to pray at the end of the busy day too.

Jesus spent time with His closest followers, away from the crowds and the demands of His ministry. He took intentional time for rest with those He led and mentored, with those who walked with Him daily. They shared meals and conversations. They sat together in homes, on hillsides, and in boats. No doubt they talked as they traveled on foot. While it was restful, it was intentional time too.

What can you take away from Jesus' witness of rest?

Rest in the presence of the One who knows your needs better than anyone. Seek uplifting time in His Word and in prayer.

Rest with people who have your best interests at heart. They know you need rest too.

Restorative rest—alone and with others—is essential for your physical well-being, mental focus, and spiritual nourishment.

Self-Care

LEANING-IN ACTION: "Hang in there!" we might say to a friend who faces difficulty. What could we say instead that may be more helpful regarding God's promises? Something like, "It's okay to let go. You are in Jesus' hands."

We are wise to create space for "margins," even on our busiest days. (As a writer, I love this word picture. No publisher would print a book with words falling off the edges of each page.) So, too, we need "white space"—margins—in our days. We need unscheduled, open space where we have time to rest and receive (or provide) personal care for ourselves.

Self-care is important; God wants us to practice healthy stewardship of our wonderfully made bodies. More broadly, He wants us to steward the whole person He created: body, mind, and soul. Where will we lean for such care? A quick scroll through social media offers numerous options. Soon ads beckon me: from mindful meditation to bath salts and facemasks; from clean eating and healthy living to massages and spa days. Even my latte and my manicure promise to mend what ails me when I'm stressed or overextended. I admit, such options can improve my mood and relax me to an extent, but can any provide the rest I really need? (Sometimes, they just remove white space from my day.) When I am weary, I need more than spa time and self-care. Any one of these activities can be helpful to some extent, but conversely, any one of them can become problematic if I use it as a substitute for soul care. How many of us search advertised alternatives for an abundant life, only to be left lacking, wanting, and weary?

My deepest weariness goes to the depths of my soul. Real rest is found in the only One who can give it. Jesus

LEAN BACK:

Ponder how you've spent free time this past week. What you do in your spare time is a good indicator of your priorities and how you seek rest. What did you read, view, or listen to? Choose one restful, edifying thing to do today.

LEAN BACK:

When might we use stewardship as a justifier for extravagance? "My body really needs the relaxation of another ____." "I'm so stressed, the added ____ is totally worth the extra ____."

reassures us, "I came that [you] may have life and have it abundantly" (John 10:10). Jesus is the Creator of rest, the only One who can fully restore mind, body, and soul. May we daily lean on Him, seeking balance that includes protecting white space and prioritizing time. Any rest regimen without Jesus is incomplete.

I SURRENDER!

We seek rest, but the world's messages keep calling:

- ❤ Earn the A!

- ❤ Get the promotion!

- ❤ Check off everything on the list.

- ❤ The more, the better.

- ❤ Failure is not an option!

So we try harder, work longer hours, and add more tasks to the daily grind. We drain our energy reserves, overextend our resources, and fill our time! We have failed to create margins in our lives. Maxed, maybe we're not living our days with gusto; instead, we're barely hanging on by a thread.

LEAN BACK:
When or where have you searched for alternatives for an abundant life? Have some of them come through for you? Why or why not?

LEAN IN #1: Sometimes you grow weary of striving. If you ever feel like giving up, give it to God instead. He holds you together, cradling you in His mighty hand. Forgiven in Christ, visualize yourself leaning against the Lord with all your weight, cradled in His care, sheltered under His shadow. Study these verses. What's your takeaway?

Psalm 91:1

James 4:7

1 Peter 5:6

Surrender your agenda. → Seek His will by His Word.

Surrender your striving. → Receive His grace in Christ Jesus.

Surrender your anxieties. → Rest in His peace.

LEAN IN #2: In the white space that follows each question below, provide personal answers that flow from your surrender from your agenda, striving, and anxieties:

How could I simplify? What needs to "go" from my schedule? Where will I reserve white space?

When does "just try harder" get its grip on me? What will help me remember to cease striving?

What's causing me anxiety right now? Where will I seek rest as I receive His peace?

LEANING-IN ACTION: Open a notebook, calendar or desk diary with hour-by-hour scheduling blocks. Where will you leave space to rest?

During a retreat session, speaker Elizabeth Bruick spoke to attendees about surrender: "Sometimes we pray about what we think is best for us; we hope badly for what we want; we give God the desires of our hearts. But God is omniscient, all knowing. He knows us, He knows our future, and He knows what we need. So, we put out our hands and say, 'I am Yours, Lord . . . I trust in You!'"

Cast
YOUR CARES

What concerns you today? What is burdening you or causing you anxiety? Complete this sentence: I'm clutching _____ tightly because I'm afraid that if I let go, something will (circle one) fall apart, end, break, leave, (other) _____.

What if God wants you to let go of it, not because He doesn't want you to have it, but because it is safer in His hands? His hands are incomparably more capable of carrying the very things you and I care about but that drain us and wear us out. Instead of fumbling for control or attempting a tighter grip, we can cast every care onto Jesus (1 Peter 5:7)! We humble ourselves under His mighty hand when we admit our weariness, loosen our grip, and lay it in His hands, acknowledging what we cannot do on our own.

> **Humble yourselves, therefore, under the mighty hand of God so that at the proper time He may exalt you, casting all your anxieties on Him, because He cares for you. (1 Peter 5:6–7)**

LEAN IN #1: Look up the following verses and write beside each reference the words that remind you of the Lord's lead in your life and your place under His care and at His feet.

> *2 Chronicles 30:8*
>
> *Psalm 55:22*
>
> *James 4:10*

Cast your burdens onto Jesus and watch His mighty hand at work. Let Him rescue you from striving and trying to take control.

HE IS IN CONTROL; you can let go.

He holds you in His hand.

He carries your cares.

Receive His rest, provision, and peace.

DRIVER ASSISTANCE

Raise your hand if you've had the pleasure of riding with a brand-new driver. I'm raising both hands, as I assisted my twins while they learned to drive. Although I tried to appear calm, I often pressed my imaginary brake and grabbed the armrest to hold myself back from grabbing the steering wheel.

Giving up the driver's seat to a learner is a humbling reminder of my desire for control and need to assist. Handing over control can make me feel panicky and restless. But what a great reminder that even when I am in the driver's seat, I'm not the person of control that I think I am. Far more challenging than controlling my car is controlling my life. If I'm driving at all, it's only because the Lord knows I could use some practice steering, braking, and maneuvering my way through life; even then, His hands guide me. Jesus has the final say and steers me clear of danger. My need for Jesus is constant.

Unlike my children, whose time and experience behind the wheel trained them to be the strong, independent drivers they are today, none of us stops learning from the Master Driver. None of us drives alone. None of us is independent; we constantly need to surrender the driver's seat to Him.

Consider . . . the continual presence of the Lord in our lives. He desires that we would be mindful of His presence as we go about our days, trusting in His lead and resisting the sinful desire to attempt to operate in our own strength. By His power at work in our lives, our desire instead is to live with a continual attitude of dependence upon Him.[26]

Strengthens our faith

* *as we seek Him thru Word & Sacrament.*

SECURITY BLANKET

LEAN BACK:

You might be familiar with the word picture that puts Jesus in the driver's seat; He takes the wheel. What kind of situation would keep you in the driver's seat? Remember, He's still ultimately in control, but when might He allow you to practice steering and braking? Why would He do that?

My children each had one and so did I. My youngest went everywhere with his blankie. The familiarity and feel of it provided soothing comfort. He could bury his face in it, wrap it around, carry it, or simply set it beside him. When he was tired or anxious, he reached for it and leaned on it, quite literally. He became so dependent upon it that he panicked if he couldn't find it.

We reach for our security blanket too, don't we?

Admittedly, I grab my phone. When I'm tired, it occupies me without my having to think too hard. When I'm seeking a distraction, I see what others are doing, via social media. When I feel anxious, I check my inboxes. My phone is a time thief, and I am not proud to say it has become my blankie. I think I need it by my side, and I turn to it for self-soothing.

My phone can be a great assistant, but I could easily let it control me. How can I hold to the cultural claim that I'm in control of my own life, when I fail to practice self-control regarding my phone?

What will help? While I know that my blankie need is an issue and I desire to do better, I confess that it has an addictive pull on me. So I go to God in prayer, seeking His forgiveness for this and anything else that has an unhealthy hold on me. I rest, confident of His grace for me in Christ! Then, I seek His help with a plan:

> **LEAN BACK:**
> What's your blankie? Is it your phone? Amazon? Gaming? A certain food? Take it to the Lord in prayer.

1. **SELF-EXAMINATION**. In my case, that means tracking how much time I spend on my phone and why. Is it helpful or fruitful? Has it kept me from completing a necessary task?

2. **ACCOUNTABILITY SUPPORT**. I solicit the help of a friend or loved one who desires my best, asks hard questions, and gives me grace too.

3. **PRAYER AND DIRECTION FROM GOD'S WORD**. I look to the source of self-control, support, and strength for the help I need. With the psalmist I pray, "Turn my eyes from looking at worthless things; and give me life in Your ways" (Psalm 119:37).

LEAN IN #2: Bring your blankie to the cross and confess your lack of self-control to the Lord. Trust that He covers you with His grace. Try my strategic plan, seeking God's help to apply the same three steps. What can you track or journal to help you be mindful of how you spend your time? From whom will you seek accountability support? Daily search God's Word for direction, strength, and help. Galatians 5:22–23 is a great place to start. How can these verses offer you comfort?

Today's technology (not just our phones and the internet, but advanced medicine, travel, and so much more) allows us increasing access to information, options, and assurances. In large part, this is quite a gift! But all this information and ability at our fingertips presents even more than a self-control issue. Ever so seductively, it can lead us into believing the lie of control in a broader sense. Control is a phony gospel; it attempts to promise us the protection that only Jesus can provide. All this information and capability don't mean we can fix everything or control what happens. We won't find power or peace in our attempts at control either. We don't need to. We have both, already, in Jesus. God be praised!

LEANING-IN ACTION: When I spoke at a recent convention, I asked the delegation to practice casting their anxieties onto Jesus with pretend fishing poles, "letting go with gusto!" and allowing God to reel in His peace in place of their worries. (See Philippians 4:6–7.)

It's All About WHO'S IN CONTROL

I'm pleased to share this section, courtesy of Debbie Larson, who wrote the following devotion. When this sweet friend and fellow writer shared her struggle with control, it gave me pause. I knew others must wrestle for control as I do, and what a gift, to receive direction from God's Word and wisdom, as shared through Debbie. Maybe you can relate to her story too.

Have you ever heard the phrase, "Let go and let God"? I like that phrase, but I'm not very good at acting it out. I tend to want to be in charge—to be in control. How pretentious of a delusion is that?

I remember a long time ago, when Scott and I lived in Texas, we put our children on a flight by themselves to spend time with their grandparents in Minnesota. I watched them smile and wave, turn their backs, and walk into the jet bridge to the plane. Scott looked at me and asked me why I had tears in my eyes. I answered that I knew family would meet them as they deplaned, but they were now on their own—I wasn't there to make sure they were safe. Scott took my hand and said, "Debbie, even when they're by our side we aren't in control. God will watch over them. He's got this."

Why do I think I am in control, ever? Why is it difficult to "let go and let God"? As I go through my day, I share all my concerns with God. I give my problems to Him—and then I take them back! I know in my heart it is my Lord in control of everything.

It's a privilege to give my worries over to my Lord, so why do I grab them back? The answer is quite simple, really. I'm sinful. In my sin, I lack trust in the One who made me His own and loves me more than I can fathom. And in these times of uncertainty, He fills my heart and mind with His wonderful words. *Trust in the LORD with all your heart, and do not lean on your own understanding. In all your ways acknowledge him, and he will make straight your paths* (Proverbs 3:5–6). Again and again, I call on the Lord, ask Him to forgive me, to strengthen my faith, and He provides His peace and encouragement.

Humble yourselves, therefore, under the mighty hand of God so that at the proper time he may exalt you, casting all your anxieties on him, because he cares for you. (1 Peter 5:6–7)

It is the LORD who goes before you. He will be with you; he will not leave you or forsake you. Do not fear or be dismayed. (Deuteronomy 31:8)

I find comfort in Scripture, knowing I am not in control. I am His child, and He walks with me and protects me as I navigate the perils of this world. He guards and protects my family.

Join me as I sit back and enjoy the flight, knowing the Pilot loved us so much that He sent His Son to suffer and die so that we would have life eternal with Him. The promise of Easter is ours.[27]

LEAN BACK:

Debbie's husband, Scott, spoke wise words to her when she struggled to let go. Personalize this portion of those words to your unique story: "Even when _____, we aren't in control. God will _____. He's got this."

Debbie recognized her sin. She was able to acknowledge and confess it to the God of grace who freely forgives in Christ. Debbie talked about the comfort she received in Scripture, the wonderful words with which God fills her heart and mind. With truth tucked in her heart, she could openly state what she knows to be true! We've studied some of the verses she shared, but as always, God's promises are worth a second look (and a third . . . and . . .) as we wrestle with control and weariness.

> **LEAN IN #1:** Read again Proverbs 3:5–6; 1 Peter 5:6–7; Deuteronomy 31:8. How do each of these speak to you when you're not sure you can "let go and let God" or when you're weary from maintaining the illusion of control?

SEEKING RELEASE

With another crazy day nearly behind me, my mind spun. It seemed that everyone wanted a piece of me, and I was glad to share. I thrive on conversation, collaboration, and conflict resolution, but at the end of rigorous days like these, I'm wiped out. I know I need relaxation and release. Where do I seek it? When I'm tired and weary, some days I wander mentally by movie streaming, snacking, or social media scrolling.

LEAN BACK:

Control. We want it. We think we've got it. And in some measure, we do. List ways or places where you exert control. When do you need to relinquish your limited control for the Lord's incomparably greater control? Pray about it.

Let's assume the best from each of these preoccupations: a family-friendly TV series, nutritious snacks, and affirming social media content. These means of release are not unhealthy in and of themselves. Are any of them *good* choices, however, when they're habitual means of escape when our soul needs more? What if, rather than relying on go-to distractions, we look to the Lord first for release and renewal of strength?

> He gives power to the faint, and to him who has no might He increases strength. Even youths shall faint and be weary, and young men shall fall exhausted; but they who wait for the

Our hearts have been made for You, O God, and they shall never rest until they rest in You.

—Saint Augustine[56]

LORD shall renew their strength; they shall mount up with wings like eagles; they shall run and not be weary; they shall walk and not faint. (Isaiah 40:29–31)

To wait for the Lord is to trust in Him—His ways, His timing, and His plan. To wait for the Lord is to look to Him for renewal and rest ahead of a quick-fix creature comfort. Doing so is not my duty—it's my delight! I don't look to my own willpower to bring about behavioral changes, but I look to His power, daily praying and asking the Holy Spirit to bring about transformation. He keeps working on my heart!

When you're weary, do you doubt God's awareness, desire, or ability to give you what you need? The verse immediately preceding the passage above from Isaiah reads:

Have you not known? Have you not heard? The LORD is the everlasting God, the Creator of the ends of the earth. He does not faint or grow weary; His understanding is unsearchable. (Isaiah 40:28)

LEAN BACK:

With great assurance, you can know that your Savior is working on your heart, effecting change in you. Incomparably greater than your willpower is His might by the Holy Spirit: "And we all . . . are being transformed into the same image from one degree of glory to another. For this comes from the Lord who is the Spirit" (2 Corinthians 3:18). Where have you seen transformation, change, and growth in your faith life? Pause to praise the One who creates these changes in you!

He doesn't grow weary. And He never grows tired of our neediness. In fact, He tirelessly gives us all we need. We can't fathom the depths of His wisdom and His knowledge of our every need. We simply cannot comprehend the limitless resource of His power! When we look to Him, the distractions lose their appeal. In joy, we can look to Him first, not condemning creature comforts that aren't inherently bad but recognizing an incomparably greater help in Him. Creature comforts may soothe our nerves for a minute, but only the Lord can soothe our souls. And how much more lasting is that satisfaction! Trust in the Lord to strengthen you. Reach out in prayer and grab a good Word before you reach for the remote or snag a sweet treat.

> **LEAN IN #2:** Grab a good Word right now! God's inspired, inerrant Word provides release, rest, and renewal of the best kind. Open your Bible to Romans 8:1–11 and read about your life in the Spirit, by God's grace through faith. Because the Holy Spirit lives in you, what does this mean for you? Meditate on verse 11 and rejoice!

LEAN BACK:

Do you have a go-to devotional that provides an affirming thought alongside a Bible passage? Maybe you have a Bible reading plan that gives you daily direction. May I suggest a Bible app and a devotional app for your phone? Have a go-to resource at the ready!

LEANING-IN ACTION: When you turn on the television, watch for a Christian message. Where do you see Christ: in a character who sacrifices for others, a display of unconditional love, good versus evil, or undeserved grace?

Yoked
WITH JESUS

You and I can lean our full weight on the One who knows that we are weary and burdened. Among the reasons for our weariness is sin. We fail God, and we fail others. That's why we desperately need Jesus, who took the full weight of our sin upon Himself when He bore our burden at the cross. Our loving Savior is with us when we are physically and spiritually worn down too, when we need rest for body and soul. Lean in and listen to Jesus:

> Come to Me, all who labor and are heavy laden, and I will give you rest. Take My yoke upon you, and learn from Me, for I am gentle and lowly in heart, and you will find rest for your souls. For My yoke is easy, and My burden is light. (Matthew 11:28–30)

Visualize yoked oxen as the first hearers would have in Jesus' illustration. A full-grown ox, in all its strength, is yoked with a calf. The calf leans into the strength of the ox beside him, who leads the way and teaches it with every step they take together.

Unpacking this passage, we learn that the Law had been like a heavy yoke the religious leaders had placed upon the Jews of Jesus' day. Perfection was demanded, but it was an impossible expectation that it could be achieved to earn salvation.

And Jesus came to them just as He comes to us today. He offered an entirely different yoke: the Gospel. He tells us to take His yoke upon us, to learn from Him . . . to lean on Him. He provides help for today and salvation for eternity.

[Jesus] knows the weight is too much for us to bear, so He takes it from us . . . fulfilling the Law perfectly on our behalf. We no longer have to labor under the heavy burden of our sin. Christ removed that burden—that death sentence—when He carried our sin to the cross and died for our sins. We find true rest for our souls through the forgiveness He

LEANING-IN ACTION: Whose big shoulders have you leaned on? Send that person a note of thanks. Maybe some big-shouldered people in your life are at rest with Jesus. Thank Him for their influence and consider who you can give a shoulder to lean on.

Let Japs are geared toward Law and not Gospel.

provides. When we are yoked, or joined, with Christ to the Gospel, He gently leads, guides, and teaches us throughout our walk with Him. He is with us now, lightening our loads as we go, giving us daily rest in Him.[28]

LEAN IN #1: Read Galatians 5:1–6. Christ freed His people from "a yoke of slavery," but in the early Galatian Church, some leaders were demanding adherence to the old laws. What yoke is Paul speaking of? What had these leaders demanded that would have the believers "submit again to a yoke of slavery"? How does Paul say people are justified and made righteous?

BIG SHOULDERS

I'm always on the lookout for local coffee companies during my travels, and recently, I was happy to find Big Shoulders in an airport hub. What do you suppose this waiting traveler did during her layover?! I succumbed to their flavor of the day. Delicious! Yes, this coffee shop called my name—then the *name* called out to me in large, bold letters: BIG SHOULDERS.

LEAN BACK:
"Stand firm!" Meditate on these words from Galatians 5:1. What is Paul saying? Don't submit to a rule or regulation or jump through a proverbial hoop to earn your salvation. You can't earn it. It's yours freely by faith in Christ Jesus. To "stand firm" is to lean fully on Christ for salvation! He's got you!

I love that. Big shoulders. It makes me think of my dad and my husband, the men in my life whose big shoulders and strong arms have carried much on my behalf; who've helped, hugged, and held me . . . and made me feel safe. Secure. I have friends with big shoulders I've leaned on. I'm blessed with sisters in Christ whose shoulders I've cried on and received comfort.

All this said, the first One who came to mind when I saw the coffee company's sign was my Lord Jesus, my Savior.

My Lord Jesus Christ

On His strong shoulder I lean. I am helped, and I am held.

In His arms, I am safe. I am secure.

By His embrace, I know I am loved, and I am saved. And there is no greater comfort than this.

When Jesus breathed His last and His shoulders slumped on the cross, IT. WAS. FINISHED. (See John 19:30.) He conquered sin and death for me. For you too. And He rose again! (Let that sink in.) 1 Peter 2:24 says it well:

> **He Himself bore our sins in His body on the tree, that we might die to sin and live to righteousness. By His wounds you have been healed.**

LEAN IN #2: How does 1 Peter 2:24 proclaim the fulfillment of prophecy in Isaiah 53:5?

Let Him shoulder your fears and your needs today. "Behold, God is my salvation; I will trust, and will not be afraid; for the LORD GOD is my strength and my song, and He has become my salvation" (Isaiah 12:2). Jesus said, "For your Father knows what you need before you ask Him" (Matthew 6:8). The apostle Paul proclaimed, "And my God will supply every need of yours according to His riches in glory in Christ Jesus" (Philippians 4:19).

Yes, He's got you ... because He's got big shoulders. The biggest, in fact.

LEAN BACK:

Think again about Jesus' yoke as He shoulders the load for you. "For My yoke is easy, and My burden is light" (Matthew 11:30). For further reflection, read the prophetic words of Isaiah 9:6. What would be upon Jesus' shoulders? Lean back and remember that He is Lord of the nations, mighty and everlasting!

Leaning on Jesus WHEN WE'RE WEAK

#Crushing It

Across social media, I see others claim they are crushing it, with hashtags like *#hustle* and *#goals*, and I wonder how they manage to *#haveitall* when I can't seem to crush anything. I wonder what's worth all the *#hustle* and how others manage to meet their *#goals* when some days, all I have is a headache. As I'm pondering this, I see a sign for sale at a store:

HUSTLE

(hus·tle) verb

To have the bravery, confidence, charisma,

and determination to persevere until you

achieve the oppurtunities you want in life

(Yes, *opportunities* was misspelled!) The more I've wrestled with *#crushingit*, the more I feel (wait for it . . .) crushed. Most days I don't feel brave, and while my determination makes a difference, that's not why I persevere. Goals are good, but when they're unmet, it's just another reason my spirit feels crushed. There is much I want to achieve, but to "achieve the opportunities [I] want in life" makes it all about me. (Besides, what I *think* I want isn't always what's best.) These realities stare back at me, and I recognize my weakness, my brokenness, and my need for His saving grace. But I receive comfort from His promises in Psalm 34:18: "The LORD is near to the brokenhearted and saves the crushed in spirit." Jesus is near; He is right here, mending my brokenness and saving me, crushed spirit and all.

Decades ago, my friend's grandma taught her that "all comparisons are odious." It intrigued me to learn that *odious* means "extremely unpleasant"; "repulsive"; "detestable"; "highly offensive." This wise woman's point sticks with me. It's terribly unfair to compare my lack of courage and confidence or my

The Lord is close to those whose hearts are breaking; He rescues those who are humbly sorry for their sins.

> **LEAN BACK:**
> Write out Psalm 34:18 and keep it before you this week. Commit it to memory and let the promises within it be a regular comfort to you. He is near. He saves!

93

fear of failure with what I perceive to be others' perfection. Only they and the Lord know their personal struggles. What a relief to remember that at the end of the day, truly *#crushingit* is not about me summoning my strength, my courage, or my determination.

LEAN IN #1: What does Scripture say related to strength, courage, determination, and perseverance? Find these or related words in the following passages and note the context surrounding them. From where does each quality come?

Strength: Psalm 68:35; Isaiah 40:29–31; Isaiah 41:10; Ephesians 3,14–19, 1 Peter 4.11 strength never

We need not fear God is with us, diminishes

Courage: Deuteronomy 31:6; Psalm 31:23–24; Isaiah 41:10; John 14:27 God strengthens

Fear not - do not be dismaid - fear not

Determination: Proverbs 16:9; Proverbs 19:21; 1 Corinthians 15:58; 2 Thessalonians 1:11

- Hope - We may plan - but God determines our path.

Perseverance: Romans 5:3-5; Ephesians 6:10–18; Colossians 1:11; Hebrews 12:1–3

Refusal to give up. Resolve, commitment

Does the Lord want me *#crushingit* with more *#hustle*? Or does He have something better in store? "God brings success to those who entrust their plans to him instead of relying on their own plans, which, no matter how sincere, are always tainted with sin."[29] With God's help, I can look beyond worldly measures of strength and success, bravery and determination to the source of everything I need. (A quick dictionary check reminds me that *hustle* actually just means "hurry." And I don't need more of that in my day!)

Jesus was crushed in our place. "He was pierced for our transgressions; He was crushed for our iniquities; upon Him was the chastisement that brought us peace, and with His wounds we are healed" (Isaiah 53:5). We don't need to crush anything because Jesus already did. At His crucifixion, death, and resurrection, He crushed the serpent's head (Genesis 3:15), defeating sin and death forever. In His strength, we truly do *#haveitall* because He supplies our every need—for today and for eternity (Philippians 4:19)!

LEAN IN #2: Below is a list of "self-talk" statements. While they are intended to be motivational, what words make you wary of their merit? How could you alter these phrases to provide Christ-centered encouragement? (I've provided starter suggestions in the answer section.)

1. "I want it. I can achieve it. I have no limits!"

2. "I am strong, courageous, and fearless!"

3. "I have the power to change my life!"

4. "I will make my dream come true!"

#NotCrushingIt

Personally and professionally, some days we see great success. Praise the Lord! He does amazing work through us! Other days, we experience limitations, roadblocks, and even failures regarding relationships, opportunities, or goals. If we have tied our worth to cultural standards, we may feel like a failure and wonder if we should just give up or if we are on the wrong track. When we don't measure up to the mantras, to standards the world has set or that we have set for ourselves, does it mean we are flawed and beyond reach? And then there's God's standard, which is perfection. We definitely don't measure up to that. On those days too: Praise the Lord! Because Christ did meet God's standard of perfection—in our place.

We have a Savior—a High Priest—who gives us our worth. He provides us with God's best. He sympathizes with our weaknesses. Just as Jesus is fully God, He was fully man. He walked our walk. He knew physical limitations when He was tired, hungry, tempted, sorrowful. He understands and fully relates with us in our weakest moments. What do we need most in those moments when we reach our limits or realize our weakness? We need His mercy and grace, and we find it before His throne.

> **LEANING-IN ACTION:** What do you see when you lean toward the mirror? Go ahead, look now. Smile at the reflection. Beautiful! Pray that you see what God sees: evidence of His grace, a reflection of His image—and it's flawless!

For we do not have a high priest who is unable to sympathize with our weaknesses, but one who in every respect has been tempted as we are, yet without sin. Let us then with confidence draw near to the throne of grace, that we may receive mercy and find grace to help in time of need. (Hebrews 4:15–16)

Jesus is tenderhearted toward us; He knows our frailty and treats us with gentleness. "A bruised reed He will not break" (Isaiah 42:3 and Matthew 12:20). Jesus perfectly fulfills Isaiah's messianic prophecy. He "loves patiently and kindly, knowing our weaknesses, communicating His Word, grace, and Spirit to us in order to bind up the broken."[30]

> **LEAN BACK:**
> What worldly standards have you sought to meet? Which of your limitations and weaknesses might God use to teach you something specific? What may He use to lead you to seek answers, insight, or wisdom from Him?

God may use our areas of weakness to show us where we have misplaced our trust or confidence, our worth or identity. He enables us to view our weaknesses as opportunities to lean fully upon His strength and show Him to the world!

BEAUTY STANDARDS

I lean toward my bathroom mirror a little too closely. I'm critical of my face because it's rounder than it used to be. I see growing evidence of my age that I've been denying. I see flaws instead of beauty in His creation of me. Cosmetics manufacturers advertise that I can look younger with their products, so I've tried several, but . . . I'm still me. My husband tells me he adores me just as I am; he thinks I am beautiful. I encourage women not to compare themselves to others, but I struggle with this issue too. What kind of beauty standards have I set for myself? *Lord, forgive me for my vanity and self-deprecation. Help me to see myself the way You do, with compassion, favor, and unconditional love. Help me to recognize beauty in others through the love of Christ Jesus reflected in me. You call me precious and beloved. Your standard of perfection was met in Christ, who strengthens me and calls me to contentment, just as I am. In Jesus' name. Amen.*

Owning
MY WEAKNESS

I can admit that I'm weak. Sometimes. To a trusted confidant, I may even be able to confess specific areas of weakness, but it is not easy. It's countercultural to admit weakness, let alone own it. Because weakness is not valued, we may be quick to cover it up or strive to conquer it. The reason I'm often afraid to admit weakness is because I erroneously equate it with incompetence. I think I will appear needy, inferior, or incapable. But owning my weakness

1. enables me to connect to others with honesty and humility;

2. allows me to receive much-needed grace from God; and

3. opens doors for vulnerable conversation that reveals God as the source of my strength.

As I seek opportunities to grow in my faith, I embrace my Savior's strength instead of attempting to summon my own.

LEAN IN #1: What do these verses say about our neediness and what God does for the humble and the weak?

Psalm 25:8-9 *The Lord will teach the ways that are right, and best to those who humbly turn to Him*

Psalm 72:13 *Have pity on us - weak & needy*

Romans 5:6, 8 *Weak & ungodly - need intercession*

Romans 8:26 *Even our prayers fall short*

> **LEANING-IN ACTION:** What you wear may remind you that you sport full spiritual armor. Your shoes can remind you that He readies you to run with the Gospel of peace to someone today. When you click your seat-belt, remember that you are surrounded by truth.

STAND STRONG

Admitting our weakness and our need for the strength of Christ does not mean we should not stand. On the contrary, we are called to take a stand for the sake of the Gospel! Jesus stood in our place when He died in our place so that we may stand in the one true faith, forgiven and free. Even now, Jesus stands before the Father on our behalf as He takes our weakest prayer and intercedes for us.

We stand up for the truth and stand strong in our convictions. We may wag our finger at those whose convictions are not in line with ours or at those we call our enemies, but let's remember the real enemy: the evil one who wages war on our souls.

> For though we walk in the flesh, we are not waging war according to the flesh. For the weapons of our warfare are not of the flesh but have divine power to destroy strongholds. We destroy arguments and every lofty opinion raised against the knowledge of God and take every thought captive to obey Christ. (2 Corinthians 10:3–5)

So, here's the paradox: a posture of leaning is also a posture of standing strong—not in our own strength but in Christ's strength! He provides us with full body armor: "Be strong in the Lord and in the strength of His might. . . . Take up the whole armor of God, that you may be able to withstand in the evil day, and having done all, to stand firm" (Ephesians 6:10, 13). The apostle Paul couldn't put it more plainly, could he? We stand.

> LEAN IN #2: Read Ephesians 6:10–17. Which pieces of the armor of God do I refer to in each description below? Write the armor piece(s) next to each: shoes, shield, sword, helmet, breastplate, and belt.
>
> *We are safe in the salvation that our Savior won for us; His victory gave us victory!* Helmet of Salvation
>
> *We are covered with Christ's righteousness and surrounded by His truth.* Breast plate-truth
>
> *We are ready to run with the Gospel message of peace in Christ.*
>
> *We go forward with His gift of faith defending us, holding out the living and active Word of God.* Sword of Spirit

LEANING TREES

I live in Nebraska, where the wind blows regularly. I've seen entire clusters of trees in the countryside that lean, creating a canopy over the prairie. This permanent leaning position, caused by the regular force of wind, could have me believe the trees are weakened, but the opposite is true. They flourish because their roots have gone down deep to find nourishment and purchase in the soil. They're resilient, thanks to the ground they grow in, and can withstand the wind.

One summer, straight-line winds blew through our small city, followed by a heavy downpour that caused a flash flood. Power lines and trees went down. When it was safe to enter the streets, my husband and son joined others in the cleanup. While massive limbs came out of towering hardwood trees, one type of tree toppled entirely. The evergreen. Too many to count were completely uprooted. What surprised me was how shallow the roots of these trees were. No wonder they had toppled! I learned that many evergreens are prolific in arid regions where they must send roots deep to access moisture. What was wrong with the trees in my neighborhood? They were planted in yards that are watered regularly. These evergreens had it easy. When that storm came, these trees, healthy on the surface, were top-heavy with shallow roots.

> **LEAN BACK:**
> What are you called to stand strong for these days regarding your faith? Describe the difference it makes for you, knowing you never stand alone or in your own strength.

handwritten margin notes: temptations / evil cloaked / Deserve death & hell / but have Lord / as our hope.

> Blessed is the man who trusts in the Lord, whose trust is the Lord. He is like a tree planted by water, that sends out its roots by the stream, and does not fear when heat comes, for its leaves remain green, and is not anxious in the year of drought, for it does not cease to bear fruit. (Jeremiah 17:7–8)

It's not enough to appear healthy if our roots don't grow deep in Christ. "Planted by water" are we whose trust is the Lord. As we grow internally, we're strengthened and prepared for both sunny and stormy days. He knows both are coming.

handwritten margin note: refinement

> The righteous flourish like the palm tree and grow like a cedar in Lebanon.

> They are planted in the house of the Lord; they flourish in the courts of our God.

> They still bear fruit in old age; they are ever full of sap and green,

to declare that the LORD is upright; He is my rock, and there is no unrighteousness in Him.

(Psalm 92:12–15)

Made righteous in Christ, we. are. flourishing. Even on days when we don't so much "feel" like we are. May we continue learning, growing, and flourishing—in worship and in God's Word—especially when we're dry, parched, and needing the nourishment only He can give. Rooted deeply in Christ, may we continue to bear fruit. (See Galatians 5:22–23.)

LEAN IN #3: Read Ephesians 3:14-19 and Colossians 2:6-7. What does each passage say you are rooted in? How are they related or even the same?

In His Love
In Christ
Rooted in faith

Self-Sufficient?

When I learned to drive, one of the first things my dad taught me was how to change a tire. We lived so far from roadside assistance, he knew that if I sustained a flat, I'd better know how to fix it myself. By the time I started college, I was a master with the car jack and took pride in helping my friends with theirs. I boasted of my independence until one winter day when my car wouldn't start and I had no idea how to use jumper cables. So much for my self-sufficiency. Fast-forward a few years and a few car models later, now I rely on roadside assistance just as much as the next person. *prideful thing*

Self-sufficiency is a best-selling idea and it's easy to see why, especially when we wouldn't want the world to know our weaknesses. A quick internet search results in a plethora of secular sources championing the strength of self-sufficiency. With books, webinars, and a prevailing spirit of individualism across our culture, we believe we can exert independence and take matters into our own hands.

"Self-sufficiency" sounds more pleasing than "pride," but sometimes they are one and the same.[31] Both assume a subtle deception that could have us fail to recognize God's power, provision, and presence in all things. Do we realize our lack of sufficiency apart from Christ? If we don't feel needy, are we any less dependent on Him? Not at

LEAN BACK:

In what areas do you consider yourself most self-sufficient? Perhaps by years of experience, education, or training? A healthy level of autonomy is a good thing, especially as we seek to be good stewards of all that's been entrusted to us—our bodies, our time, our resources, and our families, to name a few.

all. If we've fallen for the deception of self-sufficiency, we may find ourselves on either end of a swinging pendulum. On one end, accomplishments and success may lead to pride and self-righteousness. On the other end, pandemonium and failure may lead to anxiety and despair. And attempts at control prevent us from acknowledging our needs or living with humility.

Resist the deception of self-sufficiency as you rest in the arms of the all-sufficient Savior.

Even as Christ-followers, we may go about our day forgetting to think about or thank God for everything in it. And maybe we managed quite nicely, thank you very much. Doesn't this mean we have some level of self-sufficiency? Actually,

> Anything we do without active, conscious dependence on God is [by] God's grace. He is pouring out His blessings on people who don't deserve His care and don't recognize Him as the source of all they have and do. The Bible clearly proclaims we are far from self-sufficiency. Jesus says, ". . . apart from me, you can do nothing" (John 15:5). We can do nothing apart from His generous grace that allows us to function without an awareness of His provision.[32]

The culture keeps telling me, "You are enough," so why do I experience feelings of inadequacy even when I've gone to great lengths to prove that "I'm good, thank you. Won't be needing help today." I would be chasing after a lie if I believed I'm strong enough, resourceful enough, or righteous enough on my own. I would be saying . . .

To myself: I've got this!

To others: Let me show you all I can do.

To God: I'm making good choices, God! Look at me go!

But I can't pretend to be self-sufficient. Connected to the life source like a branch to the vine, I receive His power, grace, and perspective. And that allows me to say instead . . .

To myself: God's got this!

To others: Let me show you all Jesus can do for you too!

To God: Thank You for choosing me, God. Lead me to good choices and forgive me when I fail.

God is enough. Lean on Him.

LEAN BACK:
In what parts of your life do you default to self-reliance instead of fully relying on God?

ABIDE

> I am the vine; you are the branches. Whoever abides in Me and I in him, he it is that bears much fruit, for apart from Me you can do nothing. (John 15:5)

As mere branches grafted to Jesus Christ, the vine, we are completely dependent on Him for life, sustenance, strength, and growth. Apart from the vine, we are helpless to do anything of lasting or eternal value. Our good works would be for our own glory; we would be unable to fulfill His purpose or reveal His love to others. "In Him we live and move and have our being" (Acts 17:28). Because we abide with Christ by faith, we receive His power to bear fruit; we fulfill His purpose; we give Him glory!

> **LEAN IN #1:** What do the following verses, individually and collectively, say about our God-dependency? What do they tell us about our need to lean fully on Him for life, sustenance, strength, and growth?
>
> *Ephesians 3:20*
>
> *Philippians 1:6*
>
> *Philippians 2:13*
>
> *James 1:17*

The apostle John sat at Jesus' feet with the other eleven to hear Jesus proclaim, "I am the vine," and later, John wrote,

By this we know that we abide in Him and He in us, because He has given us of His Spirit. And we have seen and testify that the Father has sent His Son to be the Savior of the world. Whoever confesses that Jesus is the Son of God, God abides in him, and he in God. So we have come to know and to believe the love that God has for us. God is love, and whoever abides in love abides in God, and God abides in him. (1 John 4:13–16)

LEAN BACK:
Read 1 John 4:13–16 again. Draw a heart around every "abide" that you find. Pause to bask in the love of God, who sent His Son to be the Savior of the world! He chooses to abide in you, by the Holy Spirit.

SPEAKING OF SUFFICIENCY . . .

LEANING-IN
ACTION: Give
thanks as you go
about your day. As
you make a meal,
run an errand, or
complete a task,
praise the Lord for
the ability to do
every one of them!

The apostle Paul boasts only in his weakness, as Christ's power rests upon him. The Lord said to him, "My grace is sufficient for you, for My power is made perfect in weakness" (2 Corinthians 12:9a).

Paul begged God to relieve him of a weakness, a "thorn in the flesh," but God gave Paul a different answer than he hoped for. Instead of lamenting the affliction, Paul embraced his weakness. By God's grace, he could respond: "I will boast all the more gladly of my weaknesses, so that the power of Christ may rest upon me. For the sake of Christ, then, I am content with weaknesses, insults, hardships, persecutions, and calamities. For when I am weak, then I am strong" (2 Corinthians 12:9b–10). The Lord turns worldly wisdom upside down.

By God's grace, Paul could:

💜 Boast all the more gladly of his _____.

💜 Believe that the power of Christ _____.

💜 Find contentment in _____.

LEAN IN #2: What do you think Paul meant when he said, "When I am weak, then I am strong" (v. 10)? How can you apply this to your life and circumstances? *The less I have the more I depend on Him.*

LEAN IN #3: In Paul's Second Letter to the Corinthians, he talks about sufficiency in three different places. We are sufficient only because He has made us sufficient. What else do you learn about sufficiency in these verses? What or who is sufficient? For what purposes?

2 Corinthians 3:4–6

2 Corinthians 9:8

2 Corinthians 12:9–10

Fortress

"Let's build a fort!" One blustery fall day, two fellow fifth graders and I hauled dead tree limbs from all over my family's farm to a central location in one of our shelterbelts. We envisioned a log cabin, and began balancing, stacking, and weaving branches together. We dreamt of the protection it would provide from the coming winter wind and from imagined enemies who might attempt an attack. We would be safe in our mighty fort. (No doubt, it would double as a hiding place from our siblings too.) Late in the day, we ran out of branches and strength. Our fort walls were only a few feet high, and while we hunkered in one corner, protected from the wind, we realized our own homes were a stronger refuge.

We quit for the day, but in the weeks to come, I continued to haul boards around the farm, attempting a treehouse here, a playhouse there, and another fort in the other shelterbelt. I wanted to create my own refuge of protection from pretend enemies, a hiding place where I could hunker down, safe and secure. My attempts were weak and short lived. But imagine my delight when I learned about real forts in the Old West and, greater still, the fortified cities, strongholds, and fortresses found in the pages of Scripture. Best of all, I learned that my Lord is the greatest stronghold of all!

> **LEAN IN #1:** Read Psalm 18:2; Psalm 31:2–3; Psalm 59:16–17. Record every word you see that describes God's strength and salvation. What do you envision? And what does the Lord do, according to these verses?

Envision an ancient fortified city. The first hearers of these psalms may have looked upon or even lived within a fortress city whose stone walls protected her citizens from the enemies outside. How incomparably stronger is God, our fortress. The Lord surrounds us, solid as a rock! He is our stronghold. The psalmist repeatedly employs this powerful imagery in praise of God and as a vivid reminder of His protection and presence.

LEANING-IN ACTION: What reminds you that you're not strong enough to hold it together amid pressure? Apart from the Lord, you're likely to collapse. He holds you up and holds you together. Let everyday objects and activities remind you of your need for Him.

He alone is my rock and my salvation, my fortress; I shall not be greatly shaken. (Psalm 62:2)

As we envision the One who is our strength in weakness, we picture the fortress of protection that God provides on all sides, fully surrounding us in His care. In Christ, He is our salvation! The Lord is a strong tower, who holds us up and holds us together because we can't "hold it together" on our own. He lays His hand upon us: "You hem me in, behind and before, and lay Your hand upon me" (Psalm 139:5).

Years ago, I baked a three-layer cake. The batter rose in the baking, so when I pulled the pans from the oven, each layer had a rounded top. A novice layer-cake decorator, I stacked the layers without leveling them. The top layer sat on the rounded mounds beneath it, split in the middle, then collapsed. With gravity working against it, it was simply not strong enough to hold its own.

 The Lord steadies you by His strength on all sides. Think about the ways He surrounds you. He is present: *before* you and *behind* you, *beside* you and *all around* you, *within* you and *with* you!

> **LEAN IN #2:** In the following verses, what or who surrounds others? Who is being surrounded?
>
> *Psalm 32:7b*
>
> *Psalm 32:10b*
>
> *Psalm 125:2*

HE FIGHTS FOR YOU

"The LORD will fight for you, and you have only to be silent" (Exodus 14:14). How often have I attempted to carry the full weight of a decision or a difficult circumstance on my shoulders, only to realize my upper body strength is no match for it? Maybe I thought I could take care of this problem or that issue with enough research, self-help, and hard work. Or perhaps I look back to a stronger time and assume I can get that strength back if I will it to happen. What if, instead, I stop striving and seek stillness before the Lord, who fights for me with His incomparable might?

My battle looks nothing like that of God's chosen people as they took flight from Egypt with Pharaoh and his army chasing after them or later as they encountered other enemies. But I can learn from God's charge to the Israelites through Moses (Deuteronomy 20:4) and through Joshua (Joshua 23:10). Both included the bold reminder that God fights for His people. I may have to go to battle, but I don't battle alone or in my own strength. And He may fight for me in a way that I hadn't imagined.

LEAN BACK:
Compare the two referenced verses above. Note the personal tone toward His people: "the LORD your God." He goes with you; He fights for you; He gives you the victory. Rest in these promises, knowing God won the battle for your life; He fought against the ultimate enemies of sin, death, and the devil, and He gave you the victory in Christ, your Savior.

Every time I lean on the Lord, He proves trust-worthy, and His Spirit expands my trust and emboldens my faith. Sometimes His support comes directly through His reassuring Word. The Spirit provides inner strength that I do not possess on my own. God's Word guides my words. Praise the Lord! Other times, I receive the Lord's support through other people as He works mightily through them.

[handwritten: comes with the Sacraments]

[handwritten: ✗]

[handwritten: 40:29 He gives power to tired and worn out, and strength to the weak.]

[handwritten: Cancer]

[handwritten: Isaiah 40:31]

LEAN BACK:
Recall a time you leaned on the Lord for strength in your weakness, guided by His Word. How was God's Word your strength in every way?

When you didn't think you were strong enough to face a difficult person or situation but found a strength not your own when the time came.

When you were physically weak from illness or injury or when you caved to the ways of the world, but you received His strength for healing, to resist a temptation, for humility to admit an addiction, or in other personal struggles.

When you were emotionally or spiritually spent.

Jesus Came for THE WEAK

The Gospel is profoundly good news for all who are weak! Christ came—God in the flesh—in the weakest of ways, as a helpless newborn child. Jesus reached out repeatedly to the weak, meek, and lowly; the despised, rejected, and forgotten. Impoverished. Lame. Blind. Sick. Possessed. Diseased. Sinful. (See Mark 2:17.)

Jesus comes to us, whatever our weakness; He sees us in our sin and brokenness too. He went willingly to the cross to do what we could not. As He suffered there, others scoffed, "He saved others; let Him save Himself!" (Luke 23:35). They did not understand that what appeared to be Jesus' weakest moment was truly His strongest. It was also His greatest act of love. He became sin who knew no sin (2 Corinthians 5:21). His body was broken for the restoration of our brokenness.

LEAN IN #1: Study a sampling of the many people to whom Jesus reached out individually. As you read each account, envision how each of them leaned or knelt toward Jesus, and picture His posture toward them in response. In what ways were they weak? What did Jesus do for them?

LEANING-IN ACTION: Bring hand weights to your devotion space and do sets of arm curls and extensions between sets of Scripture. Be mindful that God's power in you enables you to be a good steward of both body and spirit.

	Who were they? In what way(s) were they weak?	What did Jesus do for them?
Luke 13:10–13	Healed by her touch & faith — had a disabled spirit	
Luke 18:35–43	Acknowledged Jesus — was sighted	
Matthew 8:1–3	Knelt before Jesus — healed / cleansed	
Mark 5:1–13	Deamon possessed completely consumed self mutilated. Cast deamon out	
Luke 7:36–50		
Mark 5:24–34		

All about forgiveness of sins.

where did the deamons go?

In her Bible study *God's Relentless Love,* author Sharla Fritz wrote:

God doesn't give up on us because of our weakness. He never abandons us because of our imperfections. In 2 Timothy 2:13, Paul says, "If we are faithless, He remains faithful—for He cannot deny Himself."

God will never just move on and look for someone else. He never gives up on us. . . . Even when we are helpless, He will continually reach out in love, hoping we will trust in the mercy and grace He extends to us because of Jesus.

God perseveres, pursues, persists, and presses on—not because we are good but because He is God.[33]

WHAT TO DO WITH A WEIGHTY LOAD

In the middle of a messy season, I cried out to God: *This is it, Lord. This trial will be my undoing. The burden is just too great, and I'm too weak for the weight of worry and anxiety over THIS circumstance that's out of my control.*

I had attempted to place the burden of my weighty situation on my shoulders.

I thought I had to carry the full load of details in my arms.

I was striving to fix it while holding huge concerns on my heart and in my mind.

LEAN BACK: Relax into the Lord. Turn over your trust. He takes the weight while you rest in Him. What weighty concerns do you carry today?

As I cried, I realized I was trembling under a weight I was unable to bear. I could feel it in my shoulders, my arms, my heart, and my mind. But I wasn't meant to hold it in the first place. I was attempting to carry what God could carry for me. I envisioned handing it all to Him, but moments later, I was grabbing it back. This back-and-forth struggle went on for weeks. A confidant reminded me that God's grace supersedes all my attempts. With the help of the Holy Spirit, I could release my grip and sink into God's mercy, where He received me and freed me, again and again.

Too big a load to carry ourselves!

How did I know He could handle it? I had His Word on it! I found comfort, reassurance, and strength in the promises of the Psalms and the Gospels.

LEANING-IN ACTION: When you lay your head on your pillow tonight, imagine that you're leaning on Jesus. Decorate a throw pillow to say "Lean on Jesus." What a reminder!

I remember You upon my bed, and meditate on You in the watches of the night; for You have been my help, and in the shadow of Your wings I will sing for joy. My soul clings to You; Your right hand upholds me. (Psalm 63:6–8)

When the earth totters, and all its inhabitants, it is I who keep steady its pillars. (Psalm 75:3)

We have visualized already a stone fortress surrounding a city. Now envision the Lord holding the very pillars of the world in His hands. The One who keeps the pillars steady keeps me steady too. He is the Rock; all other options are but shifting sand. He holds me firm when the world totters and quakes, and when I tremble. Where's my solid ground? It's found in God's Word!

I waited patiently for the LORD; He inclined to me and heard my cry. He drew me up from the pit of destruction, out of the miry bog, and set my feet upon a rock, making my steps secure. (Psalm 40:1–2)

My flesh and my heart may fail, but God is the strength of my heart and my portion forever. (Psalm 73:26)

Jesus said, "Everyone then who hears these words of Mine and does them will be like a wise man who built his house on the rock. And the rain fell, and the floods came, and the winds blew and beat on that house, but it did not fall, because it had been founded on the rock." (Matthew 7:24–25)

LEAN IN #2: In the Scripture passages above, note the actions or implied actions of the Lord toward us. What do you find particularly compelling or reassuring? As the Lord hears, helps, and upholds, what can we do in response, by His grace?

SEEK HIS STRENGTH IN A POSTURE OF PRAYER

God is our refuge, our protector, our shelter in every storm of life. Rain falls, floods come; winds blow and beat against us. Praise God, He is our Rock. He is our strength when we are weak (and let's face it, we are weak every day). We desperately need His power . . . and we receive it in Christ! He is ever present, always with us. May we seek His strength in every trouble and every stormy situation. Always. And right now.

LEAN BACK: Sometimes the concern we carry is so burdensome that we're beyond leaning; we need to be carried. The strength of our Savior carries us through. When have you needed to be carried?

Maybe our posture for prayer puts us on our knees today.

Perhaps tomorrow, we stand with arms and face lifted.

Tonight, we may lie in our bed with hands folded, eyes closed.

The next day, we'll pray with eyes wide open and hands on the steering wheel.

The Lord, your refuge and fortress, meets you right where you are. Rest in Him today. The One who spoke the world into being speaks to you through His mighty Word. The One who creates all life is sustaining yours today. The One who can calm a raging sea can calm your anxious heart. The One who spared Daniel in a den of hungry lions can save you too. The One who conquered enemy armies provides Christ's victory for you. Go to God's Word, and take your troubles to Him in prayer. He is your strength and your help.

Leaning on Jesus
WHEN WE NEED COMFORT

Hiding PLACE

I lean back into my pillow, pull the covers close, and seek sleep as I hide from the thoughts that taunt me. What am I attempting to hide from? Hurts, heartache, worries, and wanderings of my thoughts. Sometimes hiding under the covers is my way of hiding from my problems. Unfortunately, these covers don't hide me in the ways I wish they could. Hiding doesn't provide the help I need or the comfort I seek.

If sleep doesn't help, I head to the kitchen for my next attempt at comfort. I can push back anxious thoughts while pushing food in my mouth. I'm certain that with each spoonful of ice cream, I will feel better. And after that, my latest Netflix binge takes me to a different world so I don't have to face my own.

What happens when the ice cream is gone? The series is complete? The night is over and I have to get out of bed? Coping mechanisms may provide momentary relief, but they cannot provide lasting help or the peace I seek. And like so many feel-good things, they may not be inherently unhealthy. But when I overindulge, oversleep, or over-view as a comfort source, I'm left lacking and sometimes more upset with myself.

Who wants heartache, hurts, worries, or anxious thoughts? Me neither. But I'm learning that even these lead me to seek out my comfort source. My hiding place. "You are a hiding place for me; You preserve me from trouble; You surround me with shouts of deliverance" (Psalm 32:7). He covers me far more effectively than my bed's comforter. "In peace I will both lie down and sleep; for You alone, O Lord, make me dwell in safety" (Psalm 4:8). He satisfies me in a way comfort foods cannot. Though some days are filled with drama, my real life in Christ is incomparably more fulfilling than any made-for-TV movie.

LEAN BACK:

Do you have a favorite comfort food or another go-to comfort source that you crave? When is it just what you needed? When does it fall short?

Our soul finds the comfort we crave when we lean on Jesus. Even when we don't know what to say or how to pray, He knows. The Spirit intercedes for us (Romans 8:26–28). The Comforter guides us to lay it before the Lord, to commit ourselves, our situation, or our loved ones to His care, and to trust Him to work through it for good and for His glory. Our dark days are not dark to Him (Psalm 139:12). When life's circumstances take us to a place we would never choose to go, He is there. His hand guides us. He holds us.

LEANING-IN ACTION: Replace or repair something and let it be a reminder to bring old, unhealthy habits to the Lord. Ask Him to help you replace or repair these habits. He makes you brand new in Christ! Keep a mended item near you to remind you of His ongoing work in you.

LEAN IN #1: What causes you to run to or seek out your "place"? Is it a relationship challenge, a job struggle, a personal loss? Is it financial hardship or a diagnosis? Your heavenly Father meets you there. Lean on Him. He is your hiding place; He has you in His grip. Read and reflect on these verses:

Isaiah 41:10 I will help, strengthen & help you

Psalm 63:8 Cling to God

Psalm 139:10 Protected by strong right arm

The image of God holding my hand helps me understand the kind of love He has for me. It's a personal, nurturing, parental picture. It speaks to His proximity to me, His care of me, and His comfort for me.

FALLING APART

When do we need comfort? What causes us to feel like we're falling apart?

- Health complications
- Accidents or injuries
- Disrupted or waylaid plans
- Discouraging or devastating news
- Estranged or dysfunctional relationships
- Financial struggles or setbacks
- Limited options

- ❤ Limited mobility

- ❤ Global crises

- ❤ Other causes of sadness, heartache, loneliness, pain, fear, or worry

When I feel like I'm falling apart, I compare it to a crumbling mess. So I envision myself crumbling into the arms of Jesus. His arms are open wide to collect me in my brokenness. Some days I worry about the world around me when it appears to be falling apart too. Again, what can I do? I can "fall apart" into His arms.

Immanuel, God with us, holds a perfect record for drawing people to Himself in their need. Fully God and fully man, Jesus knows our hurts; He knows what it is to be human, to live in a crumbling, wayward world.

- ❤ He is "acquainted with grief." (Isaiah 53:3)

- ❤ He is our High Priest, who intercedes for us; we come to the Father through Him. We pray in His name. (Romans 8:34)

- ❤ He is Immanuel, walking with us. (Matthew 1:23)

- ❤ He doesn't leave us; He sent His Spirit as a guarantee and comforter, a promise of what's to come when He returns. (John 14:26; Acts 9:31; Ephesians 1:13–14)

Jesus meets us in our need. He grieves with us. He hurts with us. We don't have to numb it or stuff it inside; we don't need to avoid it or pretend it's not there or act like we have it all together. We can feel fully. We can trust Him to understand us, even when we can't express our feelings to anyone else. He is able to comfort us as no one else can. "I, I am He who comforts you" (Isaiah 51:12). "The LORD is near to the brokenhearted and saves the crushed in spirit" (Psalm 34:18). He heals us in our brokenness.

LEAN BACK:
Choose one or more of the truths above and meditate upon it, reading aloud the connected verse(s) and writing it here or in another journaling space.

LEAN IN #2: Look up Habakkuk 3:17–19. How does the prophet Habakkuk respond even if all sources of sustenance are lost? Next, read Daniel 3, when Shadrach, Meshach, and Abednego face the fiery furnace. What is their response to the king of Babylon in Daniel 3:17–19? *Remain faithful They will not bow down to an idol.*

God sees, knows, cares, understands, and saves. Regardless of our circumstances or the outcome, we trust Him. He is the only One worthy of our praise. He carries our full weight; we lean on Him.

May our struggles bring us closer to the Lord as He enables us to recognize more clearly the comfort only He can provide. His eye is always upon us. As we lean on the Lord, we can trust Him to provide us with the kind of comfort we need. With the psalmist, we can cry, "Keep me as the apple of Your eye; hide me in the shadow of Your wings" (Psalm 17:8).

Recline on left side to use right hand to eat, etc.

LEAN BACK:

With the help of God, what can you say when you feel like you're falling apart? When you face trials with faith, even if you don't receive the answer you hoped for?

"And even if He doesn't, _rejoice in the Lord_

"Yet, _remain faithful_."

"No matter what happens, _trust_."

Leaning Back
AGAINST JESUS

All four Gospels record events that took place throughout Jesus' Passion Week, right down to the final hours before His crucifixion. John's Gospel provides his unique perspective, including his account of the Last Supper with Jesus. The disciples were in the Upper Room "reclining at table" (John 13:23). John describes a common meal setting for first-century Israel, where those gathered around a low table would recline on their left side,[34] often on mats or cushions. John refers to himself repeatedly in his Gospel as "the one whom Jesus loved." Of course, Jesus didn't love one disciple more than another, but John humbly refers to himself this way, recognizing "that the Lord chose to love even him."[35]

John's descriptive words enable us to envision the scene, including his proximity to Jesus. He was reclined so closely to the Lord that when he sought an answer from Jesus, John leaned back against Him with his head on Jesus' chest.

> **So that disciple, leaning back against Jesus, said to Him, "Lord, who is it?" (John 13:25)**

John's question followed Jesus' shocking words about the one among them who was about to betray Him. Jesus was talking to them about the incomprehensible events that were about to take place, and they were difficult words to hear. John defines himself as the one who had leaned back against Jesus at a time when he was confused, distraught, and, likely, quite scared. All Jesus foretold that evening was too much to grasp. John needed—and received—comfort in the nearness of his Lord.

John's proximity to Jesus in that moment provides a valuable illustration for our lives with the Lord today. We may not be able to lean against Jesus physically, but we can entrust the heaviest circumstances of our lives to Him.

Don't underestimate the significance of John's posture with the Lord, especially because he chose to record that detail. John's mention of leaning against Jesus is perhaps made even more significant by his recall of it later, following Jesus' resurrection.

At the end of John's Gospel, Jesus was again with the disciples, this time on the shore of Galilee. John followed Peter and Jesus as they walked and talked, and John refers to that moment in the Upper Room. "Peter turned and saw the disciple whom Jesus loved following them, the one who also had leaned back against Him during the supper and had said, 'Lord, who is it that is going to betray You?'" (John 21:20). John defined himself as one who leaned against Jesus.

LEAN BACK:

Turn to John 13 and John 21 and read the context surrounding the verses we have read already. Note what stands out to you, especially regarding the disciple's close relationship with Jesus.

Could you and I define ourselves this same way? Like John and the other disciples, we sometimes receive difficult news. We may be confused, distraught, and scared. But we can lean against Jesus. He is so near that we can whisper questions in His ear. He inclines toward us and provides comfort as only He can.

This note in my study Bible caught my eye:

LEANING-IN
ACTION: Examine a coin during your devotion time. Find the words "In God We Trust." Ask the Holy Spirit to deepen your trust today and pray for our nation and leaders. Keep the coin near you as a reminder of the One you trust, above all.

Though a thousand other duties and relationships may cry out to you, remember that this one relationship—to Christ—has the highest priority. Like the beloved disciple, lean on the Lord and bring your requests to Him. He will hear your pleas and answer you with loving-kindness. Though a thousand other duties and relationships may cry out to Him, He will always have time for you.[36]

LEAN IN #1: When fear threatens to take hold of you, what can you do? Let these verses lead you to the reasons you don't need to fear. Mark the portions that reveal God's actions. Highlight words that show you how you can respond, thanks to God's mighty hand and by His grace. How can these promises give you comfort?

Be strong and courageous. Do not fear or be in dread of them, for it is the LORD your God who goes with you. He will not leave you or forsake you. . . . It is the LORD who goes before you. . . . Do not . . . be dismayed. (Deuteronomy 31:6, 8)

Say to those who have an anxious heart, "Be strong; fear not! Behold, your God will come with vengeance, with the recompense of God. He will come and save you." (Isaiah 35:4)

Fear not, nor be afraid. . . . Is there a God besides Me? There is no Rock; I know not any. (Isaiah 44:8) Do not be afraid, He is the Rock,

Now may our Lord Jesus Christ Himself, and God our Father, who loved us and gave us eternal comfort and good hope through grace, comfort your hearts and establish them in every good work and word. (2 Thessalonians 2:16–17)

TRUTH ON REPEAT

My friend Elizabeth spoke to me of the comfort she sought when she was overwhelmed with anxiety and fear during the recent pandemic, compounded by other issues, including racial upheaval and political polarization. As these issues weighed on her mind, she repeated simple truths to herself and to others who were distraught: "Jesus is on the throne!" "God is good!" "His Word is true!" She leaned on the Lord for the comfort that comes from His reassuring promises. Won't leave or forsake us.

> **LEAN BACK:**
> What has God done for you already? What is He doing for you today? What can you trust Him with tomorrow?

LEAN IN #2: Find these simple truths and others in the verses below. Match each verse with the following promises: Jesus is on the throne! God is good! His Word is true! Choose at least one as your go-to verse when you feel overwhelmed or anxious.

Colossians 3:1 *Hebrews 8:1*

Ephesians 1:13 *Lamentations 3:25*

Psalm 100:5 *James 1:18*

COMFORT FOR FEAR

"Lean back and squeeze your eyes shut if that helps." This was my son's advice as The Patriot's iron arms locked us in place in preparation for the Worlds of Fun ride. I'd avoided wild rides my entire life, but I was determined to show my family that fear wouldn't hold me back anymore. I wanted them to witness my newfound courage. I had calculated the risk: I could trust the steel frame. I could grasp the harness in front of me and sink onto the seat beneath me, focusing on the protective measures. No matter which way we moved, I would be secure. Right? And what a ride it was! Twists, turns, loops—right side up and upside down—and all in a short space of time. The ride was all at once scary and exhilarating! Would you believe I rode it several more times?

And isn't that just like our lives in Christ?

Maybe we've made a bold new move because we don't want fear to hold us back anymore. We've calculated the risk, as best we can. We know it's going to be a wild ride, but we also know that the Lord's iron-clad grip will hold us steady. We can lean back for security while clinging to His Word of truth. We can trust Him to keep us from falling, even when life turns upside down! Scary *and* exhilarating? Yes, but totally worth every twist and turn!

LEANING-IN ACTION: Practice stepping out in trust, but lean on Jesus first. What's one courageous thing you want to try? To say? To support? Pray, seeking God's help, then step out in His confidence.

LEAN BACK: Is there a bold new move ahead of you? Maybe you're already harnessed in the seat and ready to go. Maybe you're still calculating the risk or afraid of the outcome. Take your fears to the God of all comfort and prayerfully consider your next move.

When I am afraid, I put my trust in You. In God, whose word I praise, in God I trust; I shall not be afraid. (Psalm 56:3–4)

When I am afraid, I lean on God as my protector. He provides me with courage to face the situation or the person; He instills wisdom by His Word to guide my response; He fills me with fortitude to withstand what comes. I know I can trust Him to give me exactly what I need, enabling me to face the scary or difficult thing. I lean in, and then I step out, even when I don't know what the result will be. I trust Him with the outcome, even if it isn't what I've prayed for, knowing that by His grace, I responded in obedience, doing "the next right thing" even if it was the hard thing.

NOT *Alone*

The pilot's voice came over the intercom, reminding all passengers to stay seated and buckled as we encountered especially strong turbulence. Surrounded by fellow passengers, I was alone with my thoughts amid a sea of strangers. I watched as some passengers leaned their seats back, sank a little deeper into them, and attempted to remain calm. I wondered why the jet's jumpy motions weren't bothering me, and then I thought back to rides down miles of bumpy gravel roads. My sisters and I rode in the back seat while my mom maneuvered our car over the rural terrain with skill. As she "barreled" down the road (yes, that's what we called it), around sharp curves, and over roller-coaster hills, we had grown used to leaving our stomachs on a hilltop as we sped down and back up again. I felt safe because I trusted my mom. God had given her good sense and lots of opportunity to practice. He had our backs too. And that was just as true for the pilot and my flight.

In life, the journey is often rough, and while something could happen beyond anyone's control, not one thing happens to us beyond God's knowledge, care, or control. We can find our calm in Him; we can feel safe, even on the roughest roads because we trust Him.

There's a special kind of comfort in knowing Jesus is with me, whether I'm alone with my thoughts amid a sea of strangers or literally alone. I lean against Jesus, sinking deeper into His embrace and clinging tighter to this promise:

> **For I am sure that neither death nor life, nor angels nor rulers, nor things present nor things to come, nor powers, nor height nor depth, nor anything else in all creation, will be able to separate us from the love of God in Christ Jesus our Lord. (Romans 8:38–39)**

In verse 39, "separate" is from the Greek word *chorizo*: to separate, divide, part, to separate one's self from, to depart.[37] Nothing can *chorizo* us from God's love for us in Christ! His loving presence is constant. We are secure in His love and in His hands.

LEAN IN #1: How do the following verses illustrate the Lord's nearness and His hold of us?

Psalm 34:18

John 10:28

Author Sharla Fritz, in her book *Enough for Now*, recalls a time when she was lonely:

> Looking back, I see that season of loneliness as a gift from God. The loving Father used the time to teach me to lean on Him for all I needed. He gave me that period to experience Jesus as my "enough." Without it, I might always have tried to find enough in human relationships—and always been disillusioned. I needed a period of earthly loneliness to grow deeper in the relationship that never disappoints.[38]

LEAN BACK:
What might God be teaching you during a season of loneliness? How have you seen His comfort?

WRAPAROUND

I think about all my days alone at home because I work from there. While my home office is a great writing and work space, it isolates me from my social world. I thrive on interaction with others and find myself feeling isolated and a bit lonely. One of the things I keep in my nearby "Jesus & Me" space, as I call it, is a blanket.

With my Bible and other devotion-time goodies near me, I grab my blanket from behind and wrap it around me like a hug. I curl up in that blanket. Then I sit, and some days I lean back into my chair in a posture of prayer that tangibly reminds me I am leaning on Jesus . . . and He holds me.

I may feel isolated, but I'm not alone. I can have conversation, receive comfort, and enjoy companionship with my Savior. He knows a word before it's on my lips. He perceives my thoughts. There's nowhere I go that I'm away from His presence. The Lord reassures, "I will never leave you nor forsake you" (Hebrews 13:5). "I am with you always, to the end of the age" (Matthew 28:20). He is Immanuel, God with us.

In times or places of isolation, you and I can receive comfort from God's promise that we will never be separated from Him. Wrapped in His presence, we're not alone! We receive comfort and companionship from One like no other.

As you settle in for quiet time with Jesus, set His Word of truth before you. What else will you allow? If guilt or fear seek a spot, tell them to move along because you're making room on either side of you for grace and comfort. Expect hope to join you too. To be surrounded by this good company is to be in the grace of God, who mercifully gives, who holds you in His wrap-around embrace and fills you with His good gifts.

LEAN BACK: Look up Psalm 139:1–16 in your Bible and read it aloud. Let the words that remind you of God's presence wrap around you in comfort today.

LEAN IN #2: Curl up with Romans 3:23–24; 2 Corinthians 1:3–4; and 1 Peter 1:3 below, as you make room for grace, comfort, and hope, respectively. Highlight each of these three special guests in the verses. What does grace have to say? Comfort? Hope? What's your takeaway from each of them today?

For all have sinned and fall short of the glory of God, and are justified by His grace as a gift, through the redemption that is in Christ Jesus. (Romans 3:23–24)

Blessed be the God and Father of our Lord Jesus Christ, the Father of mercies and God of all comfort, who comforts us in all our affliction, so that we may be able to comfort those who are in any affliction, with the comfort with which we ourselves are comforted by God. (2 Corinthians 1:3–4)

Blessed be the God and Father of our Lord Jesus Christ! According to His great mercy, He has caused us to be born again to a living hope through the resurrection of Jesus Christ from the dead. (1 Peter 1:3)

LEANING-IN ACTION: What do you include in your "Jesus & Me" space? A Bible. Maybe a blanket? journal and pen? devotional or Bible study? colored pencils? chocolate or another treat?

Peering in the Past
OR FACING THE FUTURE?

Have you ever struggled to move forward because you kept looking back? Sometimes we stay stuck because of past pain, heartache, hopelessness, or sadness. We're afraid that moving forward means we will relive these emotions. So, we stand still, paralyzed in place. Trust is difficult when we stare into the unknown ahead, especially when the path directly behind us was difficult.

The enemy would love to keep us from seeking the comfort of the Lord. He would have us peering fearfully in the rearview mirror instead of looking to the Lord, who leads us toward a future only He knows. Will the future contain similar pain as that of the past or entirely different trials? Possibly either or both. But we won't face the future alone, and as we focus on the One who goes before us, we can have great expectations that He will fulfill His purpose for us.

> We could let our past make us bitter, or by God's grace, we can lean into the One who makes us better.

God goes before you. (Psalm 139:5)

He is for you. (Romans 8:31)

He fulfills His purpose for you. (Psalm 138:8)

PERSEVERING THROUGH PAIN

When I wrote *Be Still and Know*, I spoke of the comfort we receive so we can cope on our most difficult days: "By faith, I possess the resurrection power of Jesus (Ephesians 1:19–20), enabling me to face heartache head-on . . . and pain with perseverance—even when it's acute. I am not alone (see Colossians 1:27), and I believe I am richer for having faced the most difficult of circumstances, for my faith has been tested and stretched."[39]

Author Sharla Fritz can relate. She writes, "Pain isn't pleasant, but it compels me to lean on God. I don't like struggle, yet I know it intensifies my faith. I don't want to rush past the experiences

God has allowed in my life without understanding the tutorial that comes with them."[40]

And author Lindsay Hausch adds, "Life's trials can leave us on our knees; we can take the posture of prayer or the posture of defeat. On our knees, we can reach up and grab hold of God's hand as we remember our reliance on Him."[41]

> **LEAN IN #1:** Share a time when you persevered through pain, by the resurrection power of Jesus. How has your faith been tested, stretched, or intensified? Where did you find comfort? What kind of tutorial have you received? Take the posture of prayer now, thanking God for every experience, every test of faith, every trial that has led you to lean on Him, fully reliant on His grace.

My sweet friend Tamara shared her story of pain with me. Thanks be to God, it is also a story of hope. A story of leaning on the Lord. May her hope bring you comfort today too.

TAMARA'S STORY

I have learned to lean on Jesus over the past several years when an unexpected electric shock injury threw me into an anxiety disorder with frequent and severe panic attacks which I had never experienced prior to that accident. Months and years after that accident, I began feeling widespread pain and my mobility gradually decreased, despite physical therapy, working with doctors and specialists, pain medication, etc. The symptoms grew worse to the point I had to give up my full-time career of teaching for a part-time desk job, only to continue to worsen and leave me unable to work at all.

I have gone through some dark valleys of depression as the reality of the long-term effects of nerve damage and pain from this injury have stolen from my once very normal and very active life. I have had to lean on Jesus to recognize that

I have worth through Him and that He is my purpose, no matter what physical limitation I face. He is with me, and He is helping me to do the best I can, even when my sinful mind tries to tell me I am worthless and can do nothing.

In eight years, I have gone from busy, healthy, active, happy, and hard-working to disabled to the point of living a mostly sedentary life, unable to work, unable to volunteer, unable to clean my house, unable to walk through a store, and struggling to travel. I live with constant pain and mobility issues and need help taking care of myself. But thanks be to God, through the faith He placed in my heart through my Baptism, through His Word, through His body and blood given for me, I know that I matter. I know that I am more than my pain. I know that He takes my fears and anxiety and makes me whole. I know that I am more than all of [my] disabilities.

Daily, I lean on Him to guide me in the right direction for my mental and physical health care, for my spiritual care, and for my worthiness and purpose. We don't always have control over the path that life will take us down, but God has control and holds me in the palm of His hands every day, every hour, every minute, every breath."[42]

> **LEAN IN #2:** What tutorial has God provided for Tamara amid her pain? With her trust grounded in Christ, Tamara shares at least ten comforting truths. Which ones stand out to you? Maybe those are the truths you needed to read today.

REJOICE IN HOPE

"Rejoice in hope, be patient in tribulation, be constant in prayer" (Romans 12:12). No matter what comes your way, you can rejoice because you have hope even in trial or tribulation. You have certain hope in the promised Savior.

Jesus Himself said, "In the world you will have tribulation. But take heart; I have overcome the world" (John 16:33). "What a great reminder, as life sometimes feels overwhelming," said George Bruick. "We have been invited into a relationship with the One who created both the heavens and the earth. The same One who has overcome death and the grave. Let us lean on Him in every situation of life. Jesus can surely handle it."[43]

Because Jesus overcame, you and I have hope eternal . . . and hope for today. We can take heart. We can face tribulation with patience as we take everything to God in prayer. Friends, if you are facing tough stuff today, lean into the arms of Jesus; rest (and rejoice!) in the hope that is yours because of Him. Did you know that because He overcame, you're an overcomer too? "For everyone who has been born of God overcomes the world. And this is the victory that has overcome the world—our faith. Who is it that overcomes the world except the one who believes that Jesus is the Son of God?" (1 John 5:4–5).

One of my favorite devotions by Dr. Dale Meyer states, "Hope born from the fear of God makes your heart steadfast. That's why we not only fear God—that is, are in awe that He comes to help us—but we love Him and yearn for His words to hug us with hope. His hold of hope will put a glisten in your tears, because 'weeping may tarry for the night, but joy comes with the morning' (Psalm 30:5)."[44]

Even if your situation feels hopeless, you can "hold fast the confession of [y]our hope without wavering, for He who promised is faithful" (Hebrews 10:23). Lean back and let God's words hug you with hope. Repeat Hebrews 10:23,

LEAN BACK:

Far too many people are in a place where they feel hopeless. Maybe they lack a support system, or perhaps the support they once received has since disappeared. They wonder if they have anyone in their corner who cares. If that is you, hear these words of truth again: you do have hope. You may not feel it at this moment, so allow God's absolute truth to conquer every opposing feeling.

personalizing these words in prayer: "Lord, by Your grace, I can hold unswervingly . . . because You . . . ." Ask Jesus for courage to share your needs with a trusted person who can help you find a Christian organization or a church with helpful resources. They may provide help, support, or simply a listening ear. Lean on the Lord and allow Him to guide you to the type of physical, emotional, or spiritual support you need.

LEANING-IN ACTION: Choose a verse from today's reading that hugs you with hope. Then text the "hug" to a friend and write it on something you can take wherever you go. Receive hugs throughout the day!

TRUTH > *Feelings*

"Our feelings may be fickle, but we can always trust the truth." A few years ago, I came up with this phrase while leading a Bible study, and now several women recite it back to me. God's truth does not change.

God created us with the ability to feel a vast range of emotions. Feelings are a beautiful part of who we are and how we relate to God and one another. However strong the emotion we're feeling, He can handle it. But in our sin, our feelings may betray us. While we should honor our feelings and take them into careful consideration, we need to hold them up against biblical truth and determine, "Does this feeling align with God's changeless truth?" (For example, we may feel hopeless, but we have hope in Christ. We may not feel His presence, but that does not negate the truth that He's right here with us.) I cling to the promises of God's Word for comfort and grace when my feelings are all over the place.

In her book, *Take Heart*, author Lindsay Hausch says, "When we come to God in prayer, we don't have to feel His closeness to know that He draws close. We don't need to use our emotions as

LEAN BACK:

Consider your various feelings and test them against the truth. Do not shame yourself for your messy or mixed feelings. Honor them, lay them before the Lord, and release them to your Creator. There may be validity for your feelings of frustration, hurt, or anxiety. Let Him show you His truth regarding your vast range of feelings. (For example, you may feel worthless because of something you did, but God gives you your worth and says you are His treasured possession.) Examine why you may be feeling this way; you may need to dig deeper to understand an underlying reason. Allow a trusted Christian therapist, pastor, mentor, or friend to help you unpack your emotions in light of God's Word. Receive His grace!

the barometer of His love and faithfulness to us."[45] In *Emotions and the Gospel*, Heidi Goehmann writes, "God values our emotions, and not only the ones that seem pleasant or 'good' to us. They are complex gifts, each with its own purposes. Of course, we can degrade the gifts of God and misuse them. And so, perhaps most important, our emotions often point us to our need and are some of the most powerful reminders in our lives of God's redemption, restoration, and a brighter eternity."[46]

> **LEAN IN #1:** Study Isaiah 43:1–4. List all the things God has done for you and how He feels about you. His feelings are never fickle; you can trust the truth of who He says you are!

Speak truth into every situation. Maybe you can say something like this: "No matter the outcome of this situation, what do I know to be true? I know that You are good, Lord. You are with me. You are my Comforter. You are more powerful than this evil. Truth > feelings!"

> **LEAN IN #2:** Practice speaking truth into your unique situations, no matter how you feel, and let the following truths provide you with a place to start. Look up each verse and apply it to one or more of your situations:
>
> *Where it seems there is no way, Jesus makes a way; He IS the way (John 14:6).*
>
> *Though someone has been unfaithful, He remains faithful (2 Timothy 2:13).*
>
> *When we are all alone, He will never leave us alone (Psalm 73:23).*
>
> *He is our refuge in this (and every) storm (Psalm 41:1).*

REFUGE IN THE STORM

It was late fall, and I was in second grade. My father was hospitalized 150 miles from home following a horse accident, and my mother had taken my sisters and me to piano lessons after school, a mere twenty miles away at a neighbor's farm, where we had stayed for supper. A storm was brewing and it was after dark, but we headed for home. In the seat of the old family pickup sat Mom at the wheel, my big sister, Connie, and my little sister, Lisa, with me in the middle. The five-mile stretch of highway was obscured by blowing snow, and by the time we turned off the highway and onto the fifteen-mile gravel road, Mom was white-knuckling the steering wheel. As visibility decreased, she drove slowly through hills, valleys, and sharp curves. Blowing snow became a whiteout in the headlights.

From his hospital bed, Dad repeatedly called home, worried that we weren't there. My little sister was too young to understand. My big sister was a mature ten-year-old who knew the danger we were in. At seven, I whimpered in fear as Mom simultaneously attempted to concentrate, comfort us, and keep calm herself. Connie deflected her fear by teasing me: "Debbie, you're scared, aren't you?" To which I lied, "Nuh-uh! *You're* scared!" Mom crept forward and stopped the pickup now and again for a better look at the occasional road signs that marked our whereabouts. Mom knew the route well, but she didn't rely on how she felt because blinding snow has been known to confuse many a weary driver. She could, however, trust the road signs to keep her on course. Hours went by and miraculously, we managed to stay on the narrow gravel road. When we finally turned onto our lane and pulled up to the house, we ran inside, never so happy to be home.

People speak of the comforts of home, and I think my mom would agree that ours felt more like a refuge that night than it ever had before. It stood as a strong shelter in a South Dakota blizzard. Once inside, we were safe from the blinding snow and raging wind. I heard my mother close the bedroom door, pick up the phone, and weep to my father in release and relief. I'm certain his comforting words were another welcome refuge for her.

How incomparably greater is our Lord, standing as a bastion of strength, a ready refuge from the storms of our lives. Like my little sister, sometimes we don't understand what's happening. Other times, like my big sister and me, we lash out to avoid facing our own fear. Still other times, we're like my mom, bravely inching forward while attempting to comfort others. Be assured that we don't go alone; our Lord guides us by His unchanging Word and keeps us on the safe course when we could become confused or blinded in our storms. We run to Him, our strong shelter, who welcomes us to

LEANING-IN ACTION: A compass points true north. When you're lost, trust a reliable instrument and not how you feel. Consider how this truth relates to the unchangeable, fully reliable truth of God's Word.

LEAN BACK:
Share a time when you had limited visibility amid a weather storm or a circumstantial storm in your life. What unchangeable truth were you able to trust when your view was blocked or your feelings were all over the place? Pause to praise God for His changeless Word and ways!

weep with release, safely in His embrace. Miraculously, by His saving grace, we will reach the comfort of our eternal home on that day when Christ returns.

Let me dwell in Your tent forever! Let me take refuge under the shelter of Your wings! (Psalm 61:4)

LEANING IN TO LISTEN AND LEARN
→ *To Lead Well*

Listen in

YOUR HEART LANGUAGE

When I was in Tucson, Arizona, for a speaking engagement, I had the opportunity to worship with Pastor Garry and Marilyn McClure. Pastor led the entire service in Spanish. I was the only worshiper who couldn't grasp every word, but I leaned in especially closely as God's Word was read. I followed along, as faithfully as I could, in my English translation. The Gospel of John was proclaimed in the heart language of my brothers and sisters around me in the pews. Their praises were evident to me, though I couldn't understand some of their words. What a reminder that by the power of the Holy Spirit, the same Gospel is proclaimed in hundreds of languages throughout the country and around the world . . . because God so loved *the world*.

Lean in and listen: "For God so loved the world, that He gave His only Son, that whoever believes in Him should not perish but have eternal life" (John 3:16). This "Gospel in a nutshell" is likely the best-known verse in Scripture, and for good reason. In Jesus' own words, He reveals the extent of God's extravagant love for the world—for you and for me. All who believe in Christ's sacrifice for the forgiveness of their sins will have eternal life. To give this verse some context, Jesus said these precious words to Nicodemus, a Jewish religious leader who had come to Jesus under the protective darkness of night, for fear his fellow Pharisees would see him. Envision the scene with Nicodemus leaning closer to take in Jesus' profound words, likely spoken in Aramaic, a shared language. There, Nicodemus heard the truth that would set believers free.

The Gospel message is for all who

LEAN BACK:

If you serve in a foreign mission field, you may regularly hear God's Word proclaimed in other languages. Maybe you work or volunteer in a multicultural setting that has you regularly hearing a variety of tongues. Even if you only occasionally interact with someone whose language is different from your own, ask that person to teach you a few words or phrases. Be eager to learn.

receive it by faith. My visit to Tucson had me ask myself: *Do I lean in just as closely when the Word is read and proclaimed in my own language—in my home church?* May my praises be the heartfelt response to the Spirit's work in me, and may they be evident to those who witness my worship too.

HEAR HIM CALL YOUR NAME

LEANING-IN ACTION: Listen to a few well-known Scripture verses in another language(s) (Use a Bible app or YouTube.) Follow along in your English translation and marvel at the sound of God's Word in languages around the world.

Early Sunday morning, Mary Magdalene headed to Jesus' tomb to finish anointing His body, as was the custom. Finding the tomb empty with the stone rolled away, she ran, confused and bewildered, to tell the disciples. Where was Jesus? She returned to the tomb, weeping. Leaning in, Mary looked again for Jesus but saw instead two angels. Read from John's Gospel what happened next:

> They said to her, "Woman, why are you weeping?" She said to them, "They have taken away my Lord, and I do not know where they have laid Him." Having said this, she turned around and saw Jesus standing, but she did not know that it was Jesus. Jesus said to her, "Woman, why are you weeping? Whom are you seeking?" Supposing Him to be the gardener, she said to Him, "Sir, if you have carried Him away, tell me where you have laid Him, and I will take Him away." Jesus said to her, "Mary." She turned and said to Him in Aramaic, "Rabboni!" (which means Teacher). (John 20:13–16)

At first, looking through a veil of tears, Mary Magdalene did not recognize Jesus. But she had spent much time with Jesus as a faithful follower and servant. She'd listened to His voice as He spoke about the kingdom of God, as He taught multitudes, and as He proclaimed forgiveness and healing to innumerable followers. When He spoke her name, she knew who He was immediately. As we spend time with Jesus, we recognize His voice apart from all others. We are fully known by the One who calls us by name too. We are the sheep of the Good Shepherd's fold.

LEAN IN #1: Read John 10:3-4, 14-15. Because the sheep know the shepherd's voice, when they hear it, what do they instinctively do? More than knowing his voice, the sheep know the shepherd, just as he knows them. What relationship does Jesus compare this one to? Jesus Himself, the Good Shepherd, will do whatever it takes to save His fold. What was Jesus trying to tell His followers here?

We know His voice, and it grows stronger in our ears as we lean in and listen. We don't hear Him audibly as Mary did; we hear Him even better because we have His very words recorded and written that we may hear them again and again! Translated with profound accuracy into our language, we take His Word to heart, through the power of the Holy Spirit, and we can detect it apart from others' words that could lead us astray.

Notice what Jesus says of His sheep, regarding others who are not the Good Shepherd:

> A stranger they will not follow, but they will flee from him, for they do not know the voice of strangers. . . . All who came before Me are thieves and robbers, but the sheep did not listen to them. . . . The thief comes only to steal and kill and destroy. I came that they may have life and have it abundantly. (John 10:5, 8, 10)

LEAN IN #2: Lean in and listen to His voice: "Fear not, for I have redeemed you; I have called you by name, you are Mine" (Isaiah 43:1). "He calls his own sheep by name" (John 10:3). The Gospels provide glimpses of Jesus' enduring words to His people, whom He loves. What endearing description or name does He speak in each of these verses? Notice the differences among the people groups represented in this sampling. What's significant about that? What does Jesus do for each of them?

Mark 5:34

Luke 10:41

Luke 19:5

John 11:43

John 1:42 and 21:17

Jesus leads every one of us, by His grace, into a quiet space, but our space may look vastly different from that of others. Just as we are each uniquely called and gifted, so, too, we're at a unique place in our journey and season of life, with opportunities, circumstances, and relationships that are specific to us. Isn't it exciting to consider that we get to lean in to listen and learn from our

Savior? We meet Him in His Word and in His Gospel proclaimed in the Divine Service. And there He calls us to *be still* before Him.

Perhaps one or more of the scenarios below resonate with you, or maybe your journey is altogether different from these. But all have one thing in common: the need to learn at Jesus' feet:

Fractured, we come, seeking forgiveness.

Defeated, we come, seeking victory.

Empty, we come, seeking a refill.

Frazzled, we come, seeking calm.

Fatigued, we come, seeking rest.

We find all that we seek when we come to Christ, who calls our name.

- A mama struggles to find sleep, let alone a spare moment, as she nurtures a little one who leans on her for everything. Maybe she runs after older children while balancing that with work at home or work away. What precious time and place in her day can she receive soul fuel to keep going?

- A full-time student juggles class time with innumerable hours spent studying, collaborating with classmates, working part-time, and seeking a social life too. Where will she sit with Jesus for regular inspiration, guidance, and much-needed rest?

- A recent retiree is discovering a new normal, taking on volunteer work, and pursuing different commitments while learning to relax . . . when she's not traveling to see her dispersed family. How can she engage with God's Word in impactful ways?

- A single woman fills her schedule with work, family, and the community pursuits she's passionate about. She serves in her church and seldom says no. When will she take time for herself to sit with the Lord and receive from Him?

In every season, our Savior goes before us, calling us by name and beckoning us to come to Him. To lean in. To listen. To learn.

LEAN BACK:
What does (or could) your quiet time look like? Have you considered that your combination of opportunities, circumstances, and relationships provide unique ways for you to lean in, listen, and learn from Jesus?

Meditate
ON THE WORD

Now to Him who is able to do immeasurably more than all we ask or imagine, according to His power that is at work within us, to Him be glory in the church and in Christ Jesus throughout all generations, forever and ever! Amen. (Ephesians 3:20–21, NIV)

Lately, this verse has appeared before me repeatedly! An author included it in her devotion, and then my pastor shared it from the pulpit. It came up in group Bible study, and then it was mentioned on a podcast episode. I leaned closer, giving this verse more thought. I started saying it aloud, sharing it, and applying it to daily life. I've even created a letterboard with an abbreviated version for my living room. Will you lean in with me and listen closely? (Read it again.)

When I meditate on God's Word, I find more truth—something new to meditate on. And then I think about how that applies to my life, even in small, everyday ways. In the case of Ephesians 3:20–21, I want to remember that I live and move by His power working mightily in me. When I ponder this truth, how can I not jump up and down, giving God the glory?! I look at the context of these verses to be sure I'm understanding them as they were meant to be. Maybe I consider a specific situation, where I'm called to serve or listen or help. What will God do with my willing

LEAN BACK:

Marvel with me that we serve an all-powerful God who is able to do far more than all we ask of Him and even more than we can imagine! To think that He is able to do immeasurably more than that?! Wow! *Immeasurably* means we can't even measure it. Ponder that for a bit. And all of this is according to His power, at work within each of us who believe. Meditate on these amazing words some more: "To Him be glory . . . in Christ Jesus!" (v. 21). When? Now and throughout all generations. Forever (and ever). Amen.

obedience? I may never fully know, but I trust He will lead and guide me. By. His. Word.

Has there been a passage that repeatedly appears before you through various means or in more than one place within a short period? Don't dismiss it as coincidence; stop to meditate on it. Trust that God is always at work, speaking through His Word.

Invest time in your relationship with the One who created you, redeemed you, and calls you His dear daughter. Ask the Holy Spirit to create in you a desire to spend time in God's Word. Dedicate one-on-one time with your heavenly Father. Open the Bible expectantly, trusting that He meets you there—because He promises you that He will. Open it with a reverent awe. Just think of it: your Lord and Savior chooses to meet with you personally, speaks to you, and guides, strengthens, and comforts you through His Word![47]

LEAN BACK:

"I have stored up Your word in my heart" (Psalm 119:11). How will you keep Scripture before you today? This week? Think outside the box:

Take a screenshot of a short passage and make it your phone's lock screen.

Create a visual faith graphic, overlaying a verse onto a photo or original artwork.

Handwrite various verses on sticky notes and place one in each room of your home. Read them aloud, again and again, as you come and go throughout your day.

Commit to memory a verse of counsel or comfort, promise or praise.

Hold fast to the Word of life (Philippians 2:16)! To lean in and learn from our risen and living Lord Jesus is to lean on the Word of life, the Word made flesh (John 1:14). We lean in and learn via the Spirit-breathed words across all of Scripture! Psalm 119, the longest of all 150 psalms with a whopping 176 verses, praises God using many descriptors to help us see the richness and purpose for the breadth and depth of His Word, which all points to Christ.

> **LEAN IN #1:** Open to Psalm 119. In the first nine verses, you will find at least seven different words to describe God's Word. Which ones do you find in Psalm 119:1–9?

LISTEN UP!

I can still hear one of my elementary teachers call out, "Listen up!" when our K–8 country-school classroom was buzzing with chatty children. Not only did we stop talking but we turned our attention to her and listened with anticipation because those words meant something exciting was coming.

I don't know where this phrase originated, but think I'll adopt a new use of it: listen to the One seated above, at the right hand of the throne of God (Hebrews 12:2). Listen. *Up.* Some days I'm so busy I don't stop to listen up. Other days I talk a whole lot more than I listen up. But it's always time to listen up and turn our attention to the Lord because, according to His Word, He has something exciting in store: Jesus' return!

Listen. Up. Jesus said,

> Let not your hearts be troubled. Believe in God; believe also in Me. In My Father's house are many rooms. If it were not so, would I have told you that I go to prepare a place for you? And if I go and prepare a place for you, I will come again and will take you to Myself, that where I am you may be also. (John 14:1–3)

The many noises of our world would attempt to drown out His voice or distract us from it. Some noises pull us away from our focus on Christ and our trust in Him. Those noises, those voices, divert our attention and send our thoughts down bunny trails of fear and anxiety over our family, our future, and even our freedom. What happened to our focus? It went by the wayside. The evil one wants to see us distracted, placing our focus on anything but Christ. Only with God's help can we lean in again, "looking to Jesus, the founder and perfecter of our faith" (Hebrews 12:2).

LEAN BACK:

What will help you listen up with greater focus? How can you, with God's help, (1) pause from activity, (2) listen more than you speak, and (3) eliminate noise to focus on what He has to say to you? How will you listen up?

LEAN IN #2: Is there a particular verse that leads you to lean in and listen especially closely? Maybe it's one we've studied in this book and continues to resonate with you. Write it here:

Picture yourself leaning forward to listen with anticipation as He speaks His Word of truth to you.

LEAN BACK:

To what can I say *no*, so I may say *yes* to the One before me, who calls me to lean in and learn from Him? I want to receive all that I need so that I may lean into others' lives in impactful ways.

Lean Forward
AT JESUS' FEET

Luke 10:38–42 places us in the home of Mary, Martha, and Lazarus. Jesus and His disciples were among their guests. You may know this passage well, but let's take a closer look at Mary.

> **Mary . . . sat at the Lord's feet and listened to His teaching. (Luke 10:39)**

The biblical text doesn't mention Mary's posture, but the context would have us see Mary leaning in, fully focused and attentive. She was surely captivated by His presence, hanging on every word He spoke.

Normally, women weren't allowed to be seated among students of a teaching rabbi. Then again, Jesus was unlike any other teacher. He welcomed women; He wanted them in the midst of His followers and allowed them to be His students. Mary was learning at Jesus' feet. She wasn't distracted with serving; she was focused on her holy guest. Her heart was soft to receive all that He had to say.

We lean in when we are hanging onto every word too. Can we set aside the tasks, clear the distractions from our minds, and lean a little closer? What would Jesus have us learn from our time together in the Word today?

LEAN IN #1: Read Luke 10:38–42. While we often compare the sisters, Mary and Martha both learned from Jesus while He visited their home. We don't know specifically what Jesus taught Mary when she sat at His feet, but we do receive a portion of His gentle words to Martha. What did she learn from Jesus that day?

Retreat leader and fellow author Elizabeth Bruick shared this from the podium at a recent retreat: "The heads of sunflowers fascinate me. They literally move with the sun to face it all day long. They thrive in the light. May we lean in, like sunflowers lean toward the sun." She went on to share her own story of her Savior drawing her attention to Him, the One who is the light, and how He moved in her, enabling her to face the Son all day long. She said, "I found a place and a plan . . . to sit, sip on my drink, and pray . . . to read His Word and soak in all that God has for me . . . to write in my journal or write a devotion. God pursues you and me; He knows what we need. Lean in with anticipation—to listen, learn, and gain insight."

LEAN BACK:
What works for you when you seek to clear your mind of distractions so you can give your full focus to the One who knows what you need better than you do?

In every opportunity, may we be fully engaged and ready to learn, with a soft heart eager to receive what the Lord has in store for us.

LEAN IN TO PRAISE AND PRAY!

Recently, my husband and I got away for a few days and saw a breathtaking sunset, and we didn't have to wonder who created it. We DID stand in awe.

> **From the rising of the sun to its setting, the name of the LORD is to be praised! The LORD is high above all nations, and His glory above the heavens! (Psalm 113:3–4)**

LEANING-IN ACTION: Stop to pray. If you're able, step outside and stand in awe! Look at the sky and praise the One who is almighty, all knowing, always with us—omnipotent, omniscient, and omnipresent God!

May a simple sunset serve to remind us every day that the name of the Lord is to be praised—from the rising of the sun to its setting. No matter where we are or what time of day, in every way, we praise His name: our Creator, Savior, and Comforter—Father, Son, and Holy Spirit—God Almighty! If we should fear, worry, or wonder what's happening in the world, we can remember that the Lord is exalted over all the nations. His glory is above the heavens! Yes, He is almighty, all knowing, and always with us. We praise His name!

Leaning forward with heads bowed and hands clasped, whether standing, sitting, or kneeling, we assume a posture of humility and reverence before our Lord when we pray, a posture that reminds us of our complete dependence on our Savior when we bring our needs before Him in prayer.

LEAN IN #2: Note the specific posture people take in these passages and the varied circumstances surrounding their fervent prayers. Why might they have assumed this posture?

Luke 22:41–42 (see also Matthew 26:39 and Mark 14:35)

Acts 9:40

Acts 20:36

LEAN BACK:

Do you think one posture of prayer is better than others? Is there a required posture for prayer? Scripture is filled with commands to pray and accounts of people praying, but there is certainly more than one posture mentioned. In reverence, we often bow our heads and lean forward. But in praise, we may lift arms and face heavenward!

The LORD your God is in your midst,

a mighty one who will save;

He will rejoice over you with gladness;

He will quiet you by His love;

He will exult over you with loud singing.

(Zephaniah 3:17)

APPROACHING THE THRONE

Incomparably greater than any earthly king is our true King, enthroned on high. We come to our heavenly Father in the name of Jesus:

LEAN BACK:

Of the truths proclaimed above in Zephaniah 3:17, which did you need to read today? Which took you by surprise or made you marvel?

Let us then with confidence draw near to the throne of grace, that we may receive mercy and find grace to help in time of need. (Hebrews 4:16)

We come with the confidence of an heir to the kingdom of heaven, a child of the One enthroned on high. We draw near, confident because of Christ's sacrifice, which earned our undeserved status: the privilege of approaching the King directly, knowing we receive mercy and grace to help us in our need. We rest in our Savior's divine presence when we receive the Holy Meal, nourished and strengthened in faith to trust the Lord with every concern and fear. By the promises revealed in God's Word, we trust Him with our future, too, knowing that He will make all things right in Christ.

TO WIN

I'm a wannabe runner. I'm not fast, but I give it all I've got. Long before I came to love running, there was Rally Day, an athletic event cohosted by our rural schools. I dreaded this day every year because I believed I lacked any athletic ability. At the end of my eighth-grade year, I had to help represent my school on the four-person relay team. After my leg of the relay, I would hand off the baton to Scott, the only boy in the upper grades with me. I wanted to impress him, so I gave it everything I had. I ran hard and pressed on, successfully passing the baton! I don't recall how our school placed, but we did not take home a ribbon. I do recall Scott's words following the race: "Debbie, you were supposed to run, not jog."

While we may not win or even place in an athletic competition, we run the race of faith with abandon, knowing Christ has won the victory by His sacrifice at the cross. With our eyes on the Lord, we give everything we have, straining forward and running hard as we represent our Savior, as we live and give our witness for Him. May we successfully pass the baton when it's time for another to run in our place.

LEAN IN #1: A few New Testament passages refer to a race. Note the powerful imagery in words we use to cheer on our runners toward their finish lines. Mark those words or phrases, then summarize what the combined verses say.

But one thing I do: forgetting what lies behind and straining forward to what lies ahead, I press on toward the goal for the prize of the upward call of God in Christ Jesus. (Philippians 3:13–14)

Do you not know that in a race all the runners run, but only one receives the prize? So run that you may obtain it. (1 Corinthians 9:24)

Let us run with endurance the race that is set before us, looking to Jesus, the founder and perfecter of our faith. (Hebrews 12:1–2)

LEAN BACK:

As you run the race, how will you keep your eyes on the prize, remaining mindful of God's presence even when you're not reading, studying, or meditating on His Word? With His help, how can you be intentional, remembering to let Him lead? Ask yourself:

Whom will He place in my path today?

What godly response can I give as I honor that person's question?

Which decision will honor God and give Him glory?

What does God's Word have to say regarding this difficult dilemma?

What will my witness look like today? In this situation?

How can I be prepared to give a God-pleasing response when confronted with an unexpected question or challenge?

LEANING-IN ACTION: What are you running off to do today? What decisions need to be made? Before you begin, seek God's counsel and wisdom. Lean in to Him, then run with your eyes on the prize!

GOD LEANS IN

Let's take a closer look at another illustration of God's posture toward us. We know He holds our hand and shelters us in His protective care. And here we read that He bends down to listen. He inclines His ear. Yes, God leans in to listen, by His grace and according to His Word.

LEAN IN #2: The Lord hears our praise, our confession, and our cry for help. In the following verses, the psalmist asks the Lord to incline His ear, to lean in and hear his prayer. As you study these verses, watch for the reasons the psalmist needs the Lord's ear and the confidence with which he asks. Ask the Lord to incline His ear to hear your prayer.

Psalm 10:17

Psalm 17:6

Psalm 31:2

Psalm 86:1–2

I beam as I watch my pastor husband give children's messages. When the children come forward, he joins them on the steps. The children love to answer his questions and ask some of their own. When he calls on them by name, he leans in, sometimes straining to hear their small, meek voices offer a reply.

How does it feel to know that the God of the universe bends near to hear every word you lift to Him? He draws close. He leans down to listen. Although He knows what's on your heart already, He wants you to come to Him as a child approaches her trusted daddy. Crawl up beside Him, even climb on His lap, and whisper in His ear. He doesn't even need to strain to hear.

Like the psalmist, we can proclaim to whomever will listen, "I love the LORD, because He has heard my voice and my pleas for mercy. Because He inclined His ear to me, therefore I will call on Him as long as I live" (Psalm 116:1–2).

LEAN BACK:

What can you do that will help you remember God leans in when you need His ear? Call on Him now. Whether you speak aloud or whisper in your heart, He inclines His ear to you.

Christ Confidence →
LEANING AND LEADING

A few years ago, I began saying a simple phrase to myself when I speak before groups. I take a deep breath and pray just before I step up to the mic, then I remind myself to "lean, then lead." Lean first. I lean my full weight on Jesus. He leads me, and only as I lean into His lead can I lead in turn.

A strong leader exudes Christ confidence, as they lead by His perfect example while humbly remaining dependent on Him for all things. Modern-day disciples of Jesus, we learn first from Him then seek to lead well in every vocation to which He has called us and to wherever He leads.

Does your heart beat a bit more rapidly, just knowing that Jesus chooses you and appoints you to go and bear fruit? (See John 15:16.) It's a little bit scary, but at the same time, it can be exhilarating. Only as He fills you with His Word can that same Word flow through you, by your lips and with your life.

> **All Scripture is breathed out by God and profitable for teaching, for reproof, for correction, and for training in righteousness, that the man of God may be complete, equipped for every good work. (2 Timothy 3:16–17)**

By His grace, you will lead well!

LEADING WITH HUMILITY AND TEARS

The apostle Paul "serv[ed] the Lord with all humility and with tears" (Acts 20:19). Here, Paul is sharing a farewell message to the elders in Ephesus with whom he had just spent two years, teaching and training them. How do Paul's farewell words, humility, and tears provide witness to our passion to lead well, to witness of Jesus' victory for us?

> "Humility" suggests [Paul's] dependence upon God for strength and guidance. . . . He credited God's Holy Spirit for both the boldness of his preaching and the miracles

LEANING-IN ACTION: As you get dressed for the day, consider that you are clothed in Christ, covered in His grace, righteousness, and sufficiency. Pause to read Colossians 3:12–17.

he performed (Acts 19:8–12). "Tears" referred to his love for the Ephesians and the urgency with which he preached. . . .

Faced with a world that increasingly opposes or ignores the message of salvation through faith in Jesus, do you ask God for humility to rest in His forgiving love and depend on His Spirit to empower you and guide you in bold, daily witness? Aware that Christ may come again soon, do you reach out with tears because of your love for those around you without Christ and because of the urgency to share Jesus with them as their only hope for eternal life?[48]

As we lead, let's remember with humility that the Lord is our strength. We give Him the credit and the glory in all we do. We continually seek His guidance by His Word, and we rest in His forgiving love. Let's pray that He empowers us by His Spirit to this bold witness. May we pray, too, for genuine hearts toward those we lead.

A former church planter from my congregation is known in our community for saying, "Give 'em Jesus!" That's Jerry's way of reminding fellow believers to share the Good News and do it with a personal touch. Share your faith story for a most effective, from-the-heart witness. People will lean in to listen.

LEAD FROM YOUR IDENTITY IN CHRIST

Biblical identity is vital for all believers and especially as we seek to lead others. If we attach our identity to anything that's out-of-sync with our core identity in Christ, we risk waylaying those who look to us as leaders. We could inadvertently send a mistaken message. We could even find ourselves collapsing if we stand on shifting sand instead of on the Rock.

LEAN BACK:

"Give 'em Jesus!" Prayerfully consider where you will share your faith story, as you consider your relationships and regular interactions with those you know well and those you're getting to know better. Be ready to share spontaneously. What's your story? Speak humbly from your heart, trusting God to guide you. Simply share.

LEANING-IN ACTION: "Be imitators of God" (Ephesians 5:1). Follow Christian leaders: "Remember your leaders, those who spoke to you the word of God. Consider the outcome of their way of life, and imitate their faith" (Hebrews 13:7).

LEAN IN #1: Lean in to who your Creator, Savior, Counselor says you are. Summarize what He says about you in these verses:

Colossians 2:6–7

Romans 8:14–16

John 15:15

Romans 12:4–5

Acts 17:28

LEAN IN #2: Additionally, Ephesians 1:3–14 says you are . . .

You *lead* out of this identity!

GO SWINGING!

Because you know whose you are, you can truly live, lean, and lead in confidence! Confident in Christ, you can respond to Him and to the world around you. You are free to lean in and follow God's lead; to lean back into His arms; to lean forward and look up; to take healthy risks for your growth and His glory. In—back—forward—up. Sounds like you're swinging.

When was the last time you sat on a swing? As you remember, there's a lot of leaning involved. To sit upright is to sit still. Only when you grab hold of the ropes, push off, and lean back, then strain forward, again and again, will you move, leaning then stretching and gaining momentum. It's exhilarating . . . and a great stress-reliever. Our children would run straight for the swing set after school. I could see the stress of the day melt away as they flew freely through the air. I feared they would fall when they were soaring back and

LEAN BACK: Compare and contrast swinging with the posture you take in Christ, the wind beneath you as you soar through the air. Is your movement fueled only by your motion? How do you gain momentum? Praise the One who truly is the wind beneath you, enabling you to soar!

forth, but they held on and kept leaning. With that leaning came momentum, healthy risk, and release.

Let's face it: without the Lord's push, we would be sitting still. We gain momentum as Jesus moves in and through us. Lean in to learn, lean back in praise, look up to Him, lean forward to lead. Repeat. Whee!

LEANING TO LEAD

With God's help, leaning to lead means

- being authentic,

- investing in my closest relationships where trust is solid,

- being willing to be vulnerable,

- living out what I speak,

- being clear about my beliefs, and

- leading with a delicate combination of truth and love, filled with grace.

Do others see in you a willingness to reach out to someone who needs a helping hand? That might mean helping in menial ways or serving someone who has no ability to serve in return. By God's grace and with His help, we gain a heart for those who need a hand. We learn to lead with humility and by example.

> ## LEAN BACK:
> What might you add to the list above? As you consider the ways you want to lead well, remember God's grace for you in Christ. When you stumble, He steadies you. And when you fail, He forgives. Not only that, but He also gives you what you need, by His Spirit, to lean in and lead well, once again.

Ultimately, I rest in God's saving grace and so do you! We can be confident that He who began a good work in us will bring it to completion when He returns (Philippians 1:6). Meanwhile, His continual work by the Spirit enables us and excites us to see these challenges and interactions as opportunities, fueled by the Gospel of Christ!

Leaning on
JESUS TOGETHER

Together

Jesus has given you life by His grace through the gift of faith, and this by the power of the Holy Spirit. United with Christ (Philippians 2:1), together with Him, you and I are also called to be united *in* Him with one another. Our foundational relationship in Christ allows us to be in true, heart-deep relationship *together.* Because the Spirit lives in each of us by faith:

> In [Christ] you also are being built *together* into a dwelling place for God by the Spirit. (Ephesians 2:22; emphasis mine)

LEAN IN #1: Together we are the Body of Christ, His temple, the Church. Individually, we are temples too! (Ah, the great mystery and miraculous nature of God!) What does 1 Corinthians 6:19 say regarding this temple? Write the verse here: *Haven't you yet learned that your body is the home of the Holy Spirit God gave you, and that He lives within you? We are not our own!*

We receive what we need from the Lord: strength for today, direction for today and tomorrow, and hope for eternity. We continually learn what leaning looks like in specific situations as He calls us into relationship with others. Following the Lord's lead means engaging in the lives of those He places before us. We need one another. We lean on Jesus . . . together!

LIFELINE

My friend Rehema shared this startling story with me:

> In junior high I was floating down a lazy river at Camp Lone Star in La Grange, Texas. My float got separated from the rest of my cabin and suddenly I couldn't get to where everyone else was. My counselor yelled at me to float a little farther down and she would catch up.

As Rehema attempted to float farther, she soon found herself stuck in a sudden gush of water from a storm rolling in.

The wind tipped me over and I was stuck underwater for what seemed like eternity. Somehow when I managed to get my head above water to breathe, my counselor and several cabinmates had built a human chain to reach out to me and pull me in safely to shore.[49]

My friend's terrifying experience had her separated from her group, then capsized, then pulled under the stormy waters. It ended only when her counselor and cabinmates worked together to save her. In countless ways, God works through His people as we join hands and reach out together, creating a lifeline for someone in need. Only in our cooperative effort can we save the one who is sinking.

LEAN BACK:
Recall a group effort that either saved someone or provided the kind of support that could only be possible with an entire team working together, side by side or face to face. What kind of need do you see around you? What kind of team could you lead or join in a group effort to help?

Can you imagine life without the ability to lean on one another or to lean in to Christ together? Neither can I. To live side by side with one another is to do life together:

- ♥ Loving with brotherly affection (Romans 12:10).

- ♥ Embracing others when they rejoice . . . and when they weep (Romans 12:15).

- ♥ Living peaceably with everyone, so far as it depends on you (Romans 12:18).

LEAN IN #2: What can this kind of leaning look like? Who needs your affection? Your help? Your listening ear? Your forgiveness? Read Romans 12:9–18. Paul addresses the community of believers who do life together. In addition to those listed above, in what ways are we called to live this life together?

TRUST FALL OR TRUST FAIL?

Are there people in your life on whom you can lean? Even if this includes people from different parts of the country or parts of your life who you wouldn't normally see together, imagine them all with you now, getting ready to treat you to a trust fall. This crew works together to catch you as you freely fall backward from a platform and into their waiting arms—provided your knees don't buckle in sudden panic, turning a trust fall into a trust fail! Trusting in one another is complicated; it takes time, shared experience, and opportunities to build a foundation of trust.

Not long ago, I was challenged to make a quick list of memorable moments. Looking back at the list, I see a common denominator. My most memorable moments, from the best to the hardest, involved people coming together: The joy of my wedding day. Belly-laughing with friends. Playing house on the farm with my big sister, Connie. Witnessing my little sister, Lisa, have her first grand mal seizure. Meeting Cory. Giving birth. Moving to the seminary. Thank God, He created us to live this life together.

LEAN BACK:
Give yourself one minute to make a list of memorable moments. Don't overthink it, just write what comes to mind. Do you see any common denominators? Spend some time in prayer, thanking God for each person involved in those memorable moments, even the hard ones.

LEANING-IN ACTION: Try a trust fall. Ask a volunteer to face away from the group, who gather closely a couple of feet behind her. The volunteer keeps her eyes closed, knees locked, and arms crossed over her chest. Have her fall straight back into the arms of the group. Take turns. Talk about building trust.

Spending time with Grandpa as a child
rock candy walks
Senior Prom
moved to CA
1st big job
marriage - death of parents
retirement
trips w/ Mom & sisters
cancer journey
moving to be w/ sisters

Lean
ON ME

I am passionate about ministry among the people of my church and community and in my travels. So much of that ministry takes place as I meet a friend for coffee; as I pray with another person; as two or more of us walk in the Word, side by side. Confidentiality grows in small group settings as we foster friendships and nurture one another. Authenticity is possible as relationships grow and we recognize our need to continue coming together.

> We lean on Jesus, arm in arm, as we lean forward together in eager expectation.

Can we all be people who humbly welcome others to lean on us so that we can look to the Lord and lean on Him together? We're not in this alone. May we surround ourselves with fellow believers for some mutual leaning!

God uses redeemed sinners like you and me. He doesn't wait for us to get our act together before He uses us to advance His kingdom, love others, and fulfill our God-given purposes. He does, however, want us to get together to serve side by side! He provides opportunities for mutual impact. He can use our unique history, our combined interests, and our shared passion to speak into other people's situations and needs.

LEAN BACK:
Which of the following communities apply to you, where God may call you to service? Mark all that apply to you.

- ☑ Family
- ☐ Classmates
- ☑ Teammates
- ☐ Colleagues
- ☑ Neighbors
- ☑ Sports/Gaming friends
- ☑ Fellow church members
- ☑ Small group participants
- ☐ Moms' group friends
- ☐ Employers/Employees
- ☑ Close Friends
- ☐ Mentor/mentee
- ☑ Acquaintances
- ☑ _extended family / chosen_ (Other)

God will use you right where you are, in a position and in a posture that says, "I'm here to help!" How are you positioned as you recognize God's gifts to use them for the benefit of others? You have a unique usefulness, and God gives it purpose! Ephesians 2:10 says, "We are His workmanship, created in Christ Jesus for good works, which God prepared beforehand, that we should walk in them."

LEAN BACK:

What might life together look like? How might God provide for others' needs through you? It could be as simple as any of the following:

- ☐ bringing a meal
- ☐ meeting for coffee
- ☐ cleaning, cooking, caring

- ☐ listening
- ☐ advocating
- ☐ providing _____

You may be called to listen, encourage, console, or comfort, but that does not mean you can fix or force change into someone's difficult situation. Take it to the Lord in prayer. Your friend or loved one has leaned on you. Lean into the Lord's arms with every petition on her behalf. You can boldly bring it before the One who can repair what's damaged or restore what's broken. Above all, He provides peace.

I can relate to my friend Lindsay, who shared, "I'm learning to lean into the ministry of presence. To accept that where I am is where I'm meant to be in each passing moment—even if it's not where I planned to be or if I'm fifteen minutes late to be somewhere else. When I accept the presence as a gift, and practice showing up, right where I am, I get to see the divine in small moment-to-moment life. I get to carry the fullness of God with me as I trust in His provision in each passing minute."[50]

GIFT LISTS

LEANING-IN ACTION: Have a sweet treat as you meet with Jesus. Savor it, allowing your taste buds to examine the flavors and textures. Focus on the sense of taste, which God gives you, as you "taste and see that the LORD is good" (Psalm 34:8).

When a loved one asks me to make a gift list for my birthday or Christmas, I start with items that relate to my passions, interests, and personal needs. I suppose my gift list tells others a little bit about me. Incomparably greater are God's gifts to us: how He has gifted us, His children in Christ. Both the apostle Peter and the apostle Paul talk about these gifts. Our spiritual gifts vary, but we are each blessed with them so that, as we work together, every need is met. We are each uniquely equipped to impact our circles of influence, our communities.

Look at the gift lists in the following verses and consider how some match your passions, your abilities and interests, the ways you already serve, and the activities to which you're drawn.

LEAN IN: Discuss what you learn as you read each gift list. Circle types of gifts. Highlight every mention of the gift-giver. What purpose does each gift serve? Who benefits and who gets the glory?

Having gifts that differ according to the grace given to us, let us use them: if prophecy, in proportion to our faith; if service, in our serving; the one who teaches, in his teaching; the one who exhorts, in his exhortation; the one who contributes, in generosity; the one who leads, with zeal; the one who does acts of mercy, with cheerfulness. (Romans 12:6–8)

Now there are varieties of gifts, but the same Spirit; and there are varieties of service, but the same Lord; and there are varieties of activities, but it is the same God who empowers them all in everyone. (1 Corinthians 12:4–6)

As each has received a gift, use it to serve one another, as good stewards of God's varied grace: whoever speaks, as one who speaks oracles of God; whoever serves, as one who serves by the strength that God supplies—in order that in everything God may be glorified through Jesus Christ. (1 Peter 4:10–11)

EACH IS GIVEN DIFFERENT GIFTS

When Cory and I were newly married, our pastor asked us to form a Care Group—a small group Bible study—with other newly-weds. Our group formed fast friendships, and soon some of us began meeting outside of scheduled group time too. Each member was important to our little group. Each brought something unique to the table figuratively—and literally when each couple supplied a dish for a potluck. On one occasion, we were preparing to meet in our home for ice cream sundaes, and I suggested to the participants that they each bring some kind of topping. I said, "You know, like a can of whipped cream or something." Everyone took my words to heart and showed up with a can of whipped cream. Why? I had told them what to bring instead of allowing them to make their own decision. Similarly, we do a disservice to other members of the Body of Christ when we assume that everyone will serve in the same way. Each of us comes to the table with unique ideas and areas of interest. The variety helps to fulfill our needs.

As a member of the Body of Christ, what gift will you share? Your service? A talent? A message? Every member is essential for the health and workmanship of the whole body:

> For as in one body we have many members, and the members do not all have the same function, so we, though many, are one body in Christ, and individually members of one another. Having gifts that differ according to the grace given to us, let us use them. (Romans 12:4–6)

Even when our gifts are similar to another person's, they're still distinct. And when they're vastly different from another's, consider how the combined gifts complement one another.

LEAN BACK:

Revisit the gift lists above and talk about the gifts you see in yourself and in others. Focus on one of those gifts now and how you are using it already. How may you use it in the near future? In this specific context, what purpose will your gift provide? Who will be the recipient? Who gets the glory?

Comparison CULTURE

We see our own shortcomings because we view ourselves through the lens of our thoughts, insecurities, and shortcomings. How unfair to use our inner view of ourselves to consider the outer appearance of others. I deeply admire a younger woman who shares many of the same skills and passions for ministry that I do. But because she has a theology degree and I do not, I was secretly intimidated by her for a time. After we worked side by side in ministry together, I could appreciate her strengths and humbly learn from her. I no longer felt the need to compare but rather to collaborate. It was wonderful! We worked really well together, and we learned that God would use our shared and similar strengths to further His kingdom and bring Him glory!

Appreciate and value one another's uniqueness. Sometimes comparisons come in the form of devaluing ourselves or the other person because one doesn't measure up to the other according to some silly standard. Maybe she is more industrious than I am, but I'm inclined to make room in my day to listen to her. Both attributes are valuable. Both are needed. She can lean on me for that listening ear. I can lean on her for help with a task at which she excels. I'm learning to love who I am, just the way God shaped me for service, and I'm learning to love others that way too! You and I were created on purpose for a purpose. Don't silence, suppress, or stop stewarding your gifts because of insecurity, comparison, or competition.

Instead of curating a highlight-reel profile that has others watching with envy, what if we seek to reflect the reality of our

LEAN BACK:

Do you tend to compare your service to someone else's? What underlying feelings may be nudging you to compare? Take your tendency straight to God's throne of grace and receive help to recognize your gifts and others' as collaborative blessings when used together.

LEANING-IN ACTION: Members of the Body of Christ, need one another. Seek out someone to serve alongside. Who will you seek out and where could you serve together? (It will be wonderful!)

lives? Fight comparison culture. In an age of staged videos and filtered photos of every happy moment, it's overwhelming to scroll through other people's "haves" if you "have not." Let's let go of the edited version of ourselves and nurture the trust of someone who may see through us the One worth leaning into: Jesus.

GATHER TOGETHER

In the early days of COVID, we isolated ourselves for protection. While we believed this separation was the best precautionary measure, it made us wary of others. *What if that person could infect me? I don't know which professional to trust! I'm scared to gather with others.* Yes, trust took a big hit in many places. Many people lost trust in leaders, organizations, and even family members. Maybe some of us felt the only person we could trust was ourselves. How easily we became armchair experts; we did our own research, validating viewpoints that fell in line with our own assumptions or presuppositions. Maybe we searched out those who shared our views, further reinforcing our resolve to trust only those leaders, individuals, or organizations that agreed with us. Ouch.

Lack of face-to-face interaction or the ability to gather together can erode trust, especially over time. We may dream up negative narratives based on faulty assumptions when we haven't been in touch with that person for a while. I've been guilty of wondering why I haven't heard from someone; soon, I'm assuming I've upset or offended that person. When we finally see each other, I am humbled to find that what I had imagined was far from true. Maybe you can relate.

Connections are vital to relational health. We may not agree on everything, but by God's grace, we can come together in Christian love that supersedes anything that threatens to separate us. As members of one Body, we walk and we grow . . . together.

Draw a heart around the word *together* in the verses below:

> We are to grow up in every way into Him who is the head, into Christ, from whom the whole body, joined and held together by every joint with which it is equipped, when each part is working properly, makes the body grow so that it builds itself up in love. (Ephesians 4:15–16)

If one member suffers, all suffer together; if one member is honored, all rejoice together. Now you are the body of Christ and individually members of it. (1 Corinthians 12:26–27)

LEAN IN #1: What did you learn about the body of believers in these verses? What is significant about every joint, every part, every person? What happens when we are all working together? *We are joined together in love, all suffer, honor & rejoice together.*

LEAN IN #2: Jesus sent out His apostles in pairs. (See Mark 6:7-14 and Luke 10:1.) They healed the sick, proclaimed the kingdom of God, and cast out demons, in the name and power of Jesus. Couldn't they have covered twice the ground if they had gone out separately? Why do you think Jesus sent them out two by two? *Mutual encouragement & comradarie. Maybe a little protection being together.*

CLOSE COMMUNITY

God has equipped us to carry one another's burdens, hold one another together, and share one another's sufferings. We rejoice in one another's joys too. We learn to live in close community. After all, we were created for community, belonging, and shared experiences. What can that look like?

Close community might mean going beyond surface-level connections toward deeper relationships. Empowered by the Holy Spirit, we can move into greater community and togetherness in the following ways:

- ♥ *Fellowship.* We meet for many reasons. In the earliest days of the Church, "all who believed were together" (Acts 2:44). They invested socially and personally in one another, giving and receiving. They put personal preferences aside for the sake of one another's needs.

- ♥ *Meals.* We recognize God's provision, and we share it side by side, giving, receiving, and blessing. Again, a peek at the Early Church tells us, "Day by day, attending the temple together and breaking bread in their homes, they received their food with glad and generous hearts" (Acts 2:46).

♥ *Learning.* We grow in God's Word together, in praise and worship, receiving His good gifts, face to face and shoulder to shoulder. We lean in together to listen and learn.

♥ *Prayer.* We lift our praises, offer our thanks, make our confessions, and bring our needs to the Lord—together.

♥ *Doing life together!* This is one more reminder that Jesus calls us to a life of dependence on Him and interdependence with one another. We lean on Him, and we lean on one another.

LEAN BACK:
Read about the earliest days of the Church in Acts 2:42–47. While not meant to be prescriptive for our churches today, the descriptive historical text reveals the unity, generosity, and close community of the fledgling Church that would spread like wildfire! What do you take away from the Early Church dynamics as you read?

Many were being saved as they shared with each other. everything

FACING TRIALS
... *Together*

Christians across my community have come together for so many reasons in recent years. They have provided hope following a few families' devastating losses. They have helped countless flood victims. They've offered comfort and care for health-care workers, teachers, and others whose labors were intensified during COVID. We serve together in God's name; we love because He first loved us. At a recent community-wide Christian women's event, community leader Hope Freshour said, "Let us be vulnerable and authentic with one another and live as Jesus calls us to live: together in His love!"

Leaning on Jesus, we receive refuge when we're weary, strength when we're weak, help for today, and hope for eternity. Trust that He will work through you and your sisters and brothers in the faith when you face trials of every kind together.

LEAN IN #1: Read 1 Peter 5:5–10 below, recognizing that Peter wrote it to the elders and believers in the Early Church. They would have heard and received these words together. Mark God's actions and demeanor toward them . . . and now toward you. Then separately mark your actions, by His grace. What does He exhort you to do? *Humble yourselves, serve with a humble heart. Let Him have all your worries and cares.*

Clothe yourselves, all of you, with humility toward one another, for "God opposes the proud but gives grace to the humble." Humble yourselves, therefore, under the mighty hand of God so that at the proper time He may exalt you, casting all your anxieties on Him, because He cares for you. Be sober-minded; be watchful. Your adversary the devil prowls around like a roaring lion, seeking someone to devour. Resist Him, firm in your faith, knowing that the same kinds of suffering are being experienced by your brotherhood throughout the world. And after you have suffered a little while, the God of all grace, who has called you to His eternal glory in Christ, will Himself restore, confirm, strengthen, and establish you. (1 Peter 5:5–10)

LEAN IN #2: Let's unpack these verses further, in the light of our shared experience with fellow believers. Beside each bullet point, write a person or a possible situation that comes to mind, as you apply these verses personally.

> *Clothe yourself with humility toward others. Seek to honor and understand others' needs, placing them ahead of your own. (See vv. 5–6.)* Ruth

> *Share your anxieties with a trusted person. Talk through them; pray over them together. Cast them onto the Lord! (See v. 7.)*

> *Seek accountability in areas of weakness where the devil would attempt to devour you. Solicit help to resist him, ultimately in your Savior's power. Go to the Word together for faith-firming truth to combat all lies which lead to fear, anxiety, and isolation. Lies also lead us to think we're too busy to build togetherness or too proud to lean upon one another. (See vv. 8–9.)*

> *Know that you are not alone, even in your trials. Receive comfort and commiseration as you learn that fellow believers face battles and they, too, lean on the Lord for strength and healing. (See vv. 9–10.)*

> *Cling to this from verse 10: He has called you—together with all believers—to His eternal glory in Christ. He restores, confirms, strengthens, and establishes you. He gives you victory for today and for eternity.* Self

Together, we gain *endurance* for the journey. Together, we *encourage* one another in life, faith, and close community because we have a God of both:

> May the God of *endurance* and *encouragement* grant you to live in such harmony with one another, in accord with Christ Jesus, that together you may with one voice glorify the God and Father of our Lord Jesus Christ. (Romans 15:5–6; emphasis mine)

With the help of God, we can live in harmony. With Christ. In Christ. With one voice. Let's allow God to use us in one another's lives, trusting that He has a purpose for every interaction and every relationship.

LEANING-IN ACTION: Choose an activity: Have a family over for a game night or dinner. Reach out to a person who is single. Take food to a new family in the neighborhood. Join a moms group. Engage in close community . . . together!

Let us consider how to stir up one another to love and good works, not neglecting to meet *together*, as is the habit of some, but encouraging one another, and all the more as you see the Day drawing near. (Hebrews 10:24–25; emphasis mine)

LEAN BACK:

Take a second look at Hebrews 10 above. Where will you "meet together"? How might God use you to create community? What is the Lord, by the Spirit, placing on your heart that may help build close community?

Work at being helpful!

Community

Never did community feel quite so unique as when my husband was at the seminary. There were several second-career students there with their families, including ours. We were all displaced from our former communities, so we hung together and clung together. Professors' wives opened their homes to the seminarians' wives, and we formed literal circles for Bible study and prayer. One amazing mentor, Renee Gibbs, let us know we were in a safe space together. We could share our fears, burdens, and feelings of loss from our former communities. One evening, I opened my heart and out came an explosion of tears as I explained that our move to the seminary left me feeling a loss of identity. Although I knew I was still a child of God in Christ, a wife, and a mama, among other things, few knew my name, and many of my favorite roles no longer existed. This new community of women shared my pain and mourned similar losses. As we continued to gather in mutual support at Bible study and family picnics, we grew stronger together in the Lord and in relationship with one another.

Community can form when we come together for any reason. Maybe you have found community in your profession or because you share an interest with others. Your small group, sports team, book club, office, or classroom is community. Perhaps your community has formed naturally in your neighborhood, by sheer proximity! Maybe community came out of a mutual need. Consider those community groups where your witness for Christ can make all the difference in the lives of those who lack hope. As relationships deepen and trust grows, your consistent presence, words, and support can lead others to lean in and listen as you offer what only Christ can give them.

LEANING-IN ACTION: Practice community this week. Take cookies to a neighbor. Send encouragement to others in your group. Surprise co-workers with a coffee order. Trust God to lead you, according to His purpose, in your role as a member of each community.

LEAN BACK:
Maybe you have lived in the same community all your life, or maybe you've moved a lot, like my family has. Either way, you have a variety of communities within your geographic community. What's one former or current community of yours that has been especially meaningful to you. Why? Pause to thank God for the connections made within this community.

COMMUNITY OF BELIEVERS

The community of believers forms a precious community called *the Church*. I am awed every time I hear a chorus of voices speaking or singing together in harmony, yet with one voice. Romans 15:6 proclaims, "Together you may with one voice glorify the God and Father of our Lord Jesus Christ." Ahh! Together.

LEAN BACK:
The next time you're in worship, take notice of every detail you do together with the believers around you, as you respond to God's gifts to you. Standing or kneeling at the communion rail to receive His body and His blood for the forgiveness of sins. Lifting your voices as one in joyful song. Bowing your heads to pray. Confessing your sins together and receiving absolution. And more!

When the Body of Christ comes together in unity, we remember that we are one in Christ, all members of the same body. As the apostle Paul exhorts the Early Church in Philippi, so we still come together today, strengthened by the Holy Spirit, "standing firm in one spirit, with one mind striving side by side for the faith of the gospel . . . being of the same mind, having the same love, being in full accord and of one mind" (Philippians 1:27; 2:2).

Behold, how good and pleasant it is when brothers dwell in unity! (Psalm 133:1)

LEAN IN #1: In the following verses and the context around them, we learn how believers have come together in differing settings. What are those settings and what do you take away from each situation and context, especially regarding unity?

Acts 12:12 Prayer meeting
Romans 15:30 Prayer partners
1 Corinthians 1:2 Invited by God to be His people
Ephesians 2:19-22 No longer strangers — Jews & Gentiles members of God's family

FRIENDS BRING FRIENDS TO JESUS

News of Jesus' teaching and miraculous healing spread quickly; early in His ministry, and crowds formed around Him. On one occasion while Jesus was teaching, those crowds included religious leaders who had traveled from every village in Galilee and even from Judea and Jerusalem. Amid such a scene, a group of men arrived, carrying a man who was paralyzed on his bed.

The man was in need, and his friends believed Jesus could heal him. They carried him to the place where Jesus was teaching. As they neared the building, they knew they couldn't get their friend through the crowds, but they didn't let the apparent impossibility of their situation stop them. They worked together to get this man to Jesus, and it was quite the team effort.

> LEAN IN #2: Read Luke 5:18–26. Though the friends of the man may be a peripheral part of this story, they have a special role. In what unique way did these men manage to lay him before Jesus for healing? What did Jesus see in this man and his caring friends? By way of His words and His miraculous work, how did Jesus prove the religious leaders' charge against Him to be true? *Lowered man through roof. Saw their faith. Healed the man. (good friends not giving up)*

We know the man's immediate response to Jesus' miraculous healing: he picked up his bed and walked home, glorifying God. We can imagine the extent of his friends' joy. Certainly, they were among the amazed crowds of people who were filled with awe and who glorified God: "We have seen extraordinary things today" (v. 26).

Have your friends heard the Good News of Jesus? Maybe they've been skeptical, like some religious leaders of Jesus' day. Maybe they are unable to see Him on their own, like the man who was paralyzed. You know your friends are in need, and you know Jesus is the help they need. Though obstacles may get in the way, let your faith take the lead. Trust that He who is able to do far more than you ask or even imagine, according to His power at work in you, will be glorified in Christ Jesus (see Ephesians 3:20–21). Maybe your friends will even say they have seen extraordinary things that day!

With team effort, *together*, you can bring your friends to meet Jesus.

Leaning on
ONE ANOTHER

Relief

Whether you're watching Little League or the MLB, envision this: it's a great game, in large part because of the pitcher. Suddenly, his pitching takes a turn, and he walks the batter. One more pitch and another walk. He rubs his aching arm, takes a deep breath, winds up, and leans in hard as he releases the ball. This time a wild pitch. His strength is spent, and he's ready for a relief pitcher to come forward from the bullpen and take his place so the team can finish strong. The entire team leans on their bullpen, in fact. Even star pitchers don't go it alone.

Some days we can all use a relief pitcher. Even if life has been great, maybe we've been going strong for too long and we're worn out. Weary. And God provides. He sends a friend or relative who steps up, helps out, and allows us to take a break.

God also provides a helper in the person of the Holy Spirit. He is our strength, and we lean on Him every day. One of the ways He takes care of us and our entire team is through others in our lives. To continue the analogy, we are all star pitchers for a given team and backup pitchers on others. Every one of us gives and receives relief. This world and its daily demands wear us out. We need one another for so many reasons: from words of encouragement to words of hope, from practical help to prayer support, from comfort to forgiveness. We point one another to Christ. We guide one another back when we wander.

PRONE TO WANDER

"Come, Thou Fount of Every Blessing" is a hymn that has resonated with me for years. Without fail, as I sing the third stanza, shivers come over me and a lump forms in my throat. Sometimes tears follow. Left to my own devices, I'm prone to wander. How badly I need God's grace! Praise the Lord, I have godly men and women in my life who steer me back to my Savior. I look around as I sing, and I see fellow believers touched by the same words. They share the same needs. The Lord would have us lean on one another as we receive—then share—His grace.

Oh, to grace how great a debtor Daily I'm constrained to be;

Let that grace now like a fetter Bind my wand'ring heart to Thee:

Prone to wander, Lord, I feel it; Prone to leave the God I love.

Here's my heart, O take and seal it, Seal it for Thy courts above.[51]

LEAN IN #1: I learned that this stanza is connected, in part, to Ephesians 1:13–14. What beautiful promise is shared in both the hymn and Scripture? What comfort does this provide as you sing it with fellow wanderers who've been redeemed? *Our hearts are sealed by the Holy Spirit*

LEAN FORWARD FOR FOCUS

LEAN BACK:

Have you leaned on someone who led you down a wayward road? Maybe you were looking for answers and someone lured you from your foundation of faith, your biblical worldview, or your convictions centered on God's Word of truth. Pause to praise God for the grounding He gives you in the Word, for the forgiveness you receive, again and again, as you come to Him with a repentant heart for going astray. Thank Him for the people He places in your life to help lead you back. Pray for those who tried to lead you wayward, that they would come to know the truth in Christ too.

Are you seeking "one another" time? Maybe you're ready to come alongside someone and offer to listen. "Hey, you can lean on me. I'd like to be here for you." Perhaps you could use a listening ear yourself.

Picture having coffee with a dear friend in a crowded, noisy coffee house or restaurant. What do you do as your friend confides in you? You lean forward, sharpen your focus, and display by body language that you are listening intently.

LEAN IN #2: How do you (or could you) lean forward to listen to a friend when you're surrounded by noise in a broader sense? When work, social media, extra curriculars, and other commitments vie for your attention from every direction, when your mind is distracted by your to-do list or the clock? *listen without being distracted.*

May we always strive to love well by listening well. Here are few things to help us learn along the way:

- ❤ Enter the conversation with genuine curiosity.

- ❤ Seek clarification. Respond with, "I hear you saying ___. Is that correct?"

- ❤ Desire to see the other person's perspective, even if you disagree. Seek to understand.

- ❤ Let your words "be gracious, seasoned with salt, so that you may know how you ought to answer" (Colossians 4:6).

May we also learn to be

- ❤ available, not too busy to meet (with reasonable exceptions);

- ❤ prayerful, asking for God's guidance by the Spirit before we meet;

- ❤ fully present and not distracted by other things;

- ❤ intentional with our time, without rushing to get our own words in;

- ❤ purposeful in our time, not limited to superficial conversation; and

- ❤ approachable, not distant or keeping the other person at arm's length.

LEANING-IN ACTION: Bring a beverage of choice to your study time today. As you sip, remember your greater thirst for the living Word. Envision the overflowing gifts of God to you, including friends and opportunities to connect with them and share His love.

Keep in mind the image of leaning forward as we look at "one anothers" in Scripture throughout the rest of this chapter. What do these examples tell us? There are more than thirty-five "one another" commands in the New Testament, and some appear multiple times. Hint: Love is mentioned more than any other!

LEAN BACK: What could you add or personalize, regarding either of these lists?

Love
ONE ANOTHER

A new commandment I give to you, that you love one another: just as I have loved you, you also are to love one another. By this all people will know that you are My disciples, if you have love for one another. (John 13:34–35)

A lot of people tell us to love one another, but love based on someone else's idea of love is fickle. Love based on our sheer resolve to love will be frail. When God says, "Love one another," He gives us His Word and His power to do so! "God is love, and whoever abides in love abides in God, and God abides in him" (1 John 4:16). Jesus said, "As the Father has loved Me, so have I loved you. Abide in My love" (John 15:9).

Love is who God is. Love is what He gives. His perfect love led Him to send His Son to the cross to take the punishment for our lack of love. Mysteriously, miraculously, He worked faith in our hearts by the Spirit's power, so that we—chosen, redeemed, and loved by God in Christ—may abound and abide in the same love for one another. Incredible!

LEAN BACK:
How do you abide with others in your love for them? Consider how often your abiding presence has spoken even clearer or louder than your words. Prayerfully consider who could use some time with you this week.

Loving one another is such a privilege. Because we abide in Christ by faith, we can love as He does. Jesus' words in Mark 12 cover every one of God's commands because all fall under the headship of love: "You shall love the Lord your God with all your heart and with all your soul and with all your mind and with all your strength.' . . . 'You shall love your neighbor as yourself.' There is no other commandment greater than these" (vv. 30–31). Only by God's grace do "we love because He first loved us" (1 John 4:19).

LEAN IN #1: At least twenty times across the New Testament, we are encouraged to love one another. The following is just a sampling. What special truths and helpful phrases do you find?

Romans 12:10 Show respect & affection

1 Thessalonians 3:12 God enables me to increase love

1 Peter 4:8 love even when difficult - covers lot of Sins

1 John 4:7–12 God sent His son, thru love for us
— God is Love —

Jesus said, "This is My commandment, that you love one another as I have loved you. Greater love has no one than this, that someone lay down his life for his friends" (John 15:12–13). Truly, there is no greater love than the sacrificial love of Jesus, who lay down His life for the sins of the entire world: for all whom He calls friends, for you and me. By His grace, we can love one another with the same selfless, serving, sacrificial love.

IMITATORS

> Be imitators of God, as beloved children. And walk in love, as Christ loved us and gave Himself up for us, a fragrant offering and sacrifice to God. (Ephesians 5:1–2)

The beloved child of my Father, I want to imitate Him at every turn. I want to walk in love as He does. I want to love others as Jesus loves me.

As my friend Sarah and I were swapping stories recently, she told me that I imitate other people "uncannily well" when I speak warmly of them and share their wisdom or humor. She said she could practically hear and see our mutual friends through me. Wow—I had no idea! I hope I've honored these friends with my heartfelt imitations. I want to imitate or emulate a friend's good qualities, wise words, and winsome mannerisms. I want to lean in so closely that I become a student of those I seek to imitate.

LEAN IN #2: As the apostle Paul taught, he humbly sought not to draw attention to himself but to Christ's work in him. What does he encourage believers to do? Read 1 Corinthians

11:1. Of course, the Son of God perfectly imitated the Father. What does Jesus say in John 5:19? While we cannot imitate our heavenly Father perfectly, what do Jesus' words remind us about our own walk with Him? *We can do nothing on our own. But can thru grace.*

Can you and I lean in so closely to Jesus that we imitate His voice, character, qualities, compassion, and care? By God's grace, may we remember His words and observe His actions so well that we copy them with our lips and with our lives! I hope others can say that I imitate Christ "uncannily well," that they may hear and see Him in me. While I'm a work-in-progress, I know that the One who began a good work in me will bring it to completion when He returns (see Philippians 1:6).

Part of imitating Jesus means loving those whom He loves. We don't have to muster up love on our own. The Spirit lives in us, enabling us to love as He does. Jesus loved those whom others avoided; He loved without limits; He loved even those who refused Him. Although there are many more ways we could describe Jesus' love, ponder these as you answer the following questions.

LEAN BACK:

What does sacrificial love look like? Where will you "walk in love" today? Who and how are you loving like Jesus today, by God's grace?

Loving those God loves

Be Kind to One Another
AND FORGIVE ONE ANOTHER

Jesus in the center of all relationships

> Be kind to one another, tenderhearted, forgiving one another, as God in Christ forgave you. (Ephesians 4:32)

Kindness sounds straightforward and simple. But then we think of a person we're struggling with. Maybe someone's words have us feeling defensive or hurt. Or there is someone who doesn't even desire our forgiveness. How hard it can be to show kindness, let alone forgive.

When I'm feeling this way, I find it helpful to remember who and whose I am: formerly separated from God by my sin, I am a new creation in Christ (2 Corinthians 5:17). *"As God in Christ forgave you."* I didn't deserve it, but He cleansed my sins in Christ. With God's help, I'm able to look at conflict in a different light as I ask myself, *Who am I?* I am a child of God, dearly and unconditionally loved. Who is the person I'm in conflict with? She is also someone for whom Christ died.

Remembering our identity and worth can make all the difference in how we're able to treat the person who hurt us or how we

LEAN BACK:

Recall a conflict or disagreement that is still bothering you. Surrender it to God. Ask for His strength to let go and to seek reconciliation. Ask for His help to love, despite _____, in the midst of _____, no matter what. And talk to the Lord:

"God, help me to view myself and (name) as You view each of us. Forgive me for being critical of (name), your chosen, redeemed child. Give me patience and Your love for (name)."

handle a sensitive situation. Seeking God's power by the Holy Spirit, may we forgive others, show them kindness, and approach every person with a tender heart, loving like Jesus does.

In response to Christ's saving grace and sacrificial love, and by His work in us, we can

- ♥ be kind—a humble response can quickly cool a heated conversation;

- ♥ be tenderhearted—a softened heart toward others enables us to earnestly seek understanding, listen with compassion, and build better relationships; and

- ♥ be forgiving—extending forgiveness provides a powerful witness and opportunities for healing and reconciliation.

Confess your sins to one another and pray for one another. (James 5:16)

LEAN BACK:

Concerning a specific situation, ask yourself:

What's the next kind thing I can say or do, regarding this person or situation?

How can I respond to his words or actions in Christ's love?

Where can I give her grace?

MENTOR AND FRIEND

I'll never forget when a younger mama asked if I would prayerfully consider becoming a mentor to her. She was courageous to reach out to me and asked if she could lean on me for advice and wisdom that I may have by years of experience. We were merely acquaintances at the time, but I was humbled that she had thought of me, and I accepted her offer. What began as a mentoring relationship has blossomed into a broader, deeper friendship. I believe that she mentors me in unique ways, just as I mentor her. We confess personal struggles to each other, encourage each other, listen to each other's highs and lows, and send prayer requests to each other.

PERSONAL PRAYER

Our family farm was a mere sixty-five miles from the town where my sister and I attended high school. We couldn't consider a daily commute, so we each, in turn, sought a host family to house us during the week. The Lord guided my host family straight to me through mutual friends, and my years in Steve and Deb's home were amazing. Their witness for Christ was as daily as it was compelling. I stepped out of my room each morning to see Steve leaning over God's Word before work. I held hands with their family as we leaned in together over the table for prayer. I overheard them praying many evenings, and late one night, I heard them crying out to God for me. They knew I was struggling socially, and I could tell that Deb was in tears as she lifted me to the Lord. Not only did God answers their prayers, but He used their witness to impact my faith in such a way that I still remember that prayer today.

TEACH AND ADMONISH ONE ANOTHER

> Let the word of Christ dwell in you richly, teaching and admonishing one another in all wisdom, singing psalms and hymns and spiritual songs, with thankfulness in your hearts to God. (Colossians 3:16)

I lean on my friend for words of wisdom. She leans on me for help. We lean on each other, hold each other accountable, and point each other to Christ. We lean in and receive God's good gifts. The Spirit works powerfully through the Word, in our Baptism, and at the Lord's Table. We come alongside other brothers and sisters, link arms with them, and show them that same need to lean in, walking together in Christ.

> LEAN IN: Look up Galatians 6:1–2 and Hebrews 3:13, citing words similar to "admonish" above. How do these verses relate and offer additional insight? Do you find some directives more difficult than others?

Sometimes, I need the accountability of another person to help me stay on task or persevere in a positive direction. Other times, I could use a helping hand to steer me away from a weakness. While I cringe as I consider these needs, I'm comforted by God's

LEANING-IN ACTION: With a specific friend in mind, prepare a list of God's promises relating to a challenge or opportunity your friend is facing. Send the promises to your friend, along with a note and a prayer from you.

direction in Christ. With His help, I earnestly seek admonishment from a trusted friend. It's humbling to be called-to-question or challenged, but without accountability, I could be deceived by sin. I need someone to speak truth to me in love and grace (Ephesians 4:15). I need someone who will "restore [me] in a spirit of gentleness" (Galatians 6:1). I pray that we may "exhort one another every day" (Hebrews 3:13).

Will you allow someone to get close enough to truly see you and know you? To call you up and call you out? Seek a trustworthy person with whom you already share a healthy relationship. Engage in honest conversation; "bear one another's burdens" (Galatians 6:2). Commit to this kind of leaning, where you can give that person permission to hold you accountable for your words and actions, your choices and priorities. "Iron sharpens iron, and one man sharpens another" (Proverbs 27:17).

LEAN BACK:

Maybe you already have an accountability partner. Take to heart Galatians 6:2, "Bear one another's burdens," and consider which of you is carrying the heavier load today. Which of you could do some burden-carrying for the other, and what might that look like?

Comfort
ONE ANOTHER

Comfort one another, agree with one another, live in peace; and the God of love and peace will be with you. (2 Corinthians 13:11)

A MOTHER'S COMFORT

I believe a mother instinctively wants to comfort her children; God gave her a heart and hands to nurture them as they grow. When I wrote *Raising Godly Girls*, my sweet Courtney had just passed her teen years, and our relationship guided much of what I wrote, including these words about comfort:

> Maybe [your child] is crying out, "Why me, God? I didn't ask for this. Why have You allowed this?" And perhaps all she sees is the apparent impossibility of her situation, the unfairness of it, or the pain or frustration in it. Be gentle. . . . Listen more than you speak. Ask God for timing and discernment as you offer the very real comfort of your presence, and even better, the reassuring truth from His Word—not offered tritely with a nonchalant "this too shall pass," but with sincerity that reveals your own trust in God, in spite of and in the midst of difficult circumstances. . . . Encourage her to talk to Jesus, and approach His . . . throne of grace with her. Seek His help, comfort, deliverance, and peace. The Lord tenderly tells both of you, "Call upon Me in the day of trouble; I will deliver you, and you shall glorify Me" (Psalm 50:15).[52]

LETTER A

Lee and Sylvia were known for leaning on one another in more ways than one. When my husband took a call to their church, they'd already enjoyed more than fifty years of marriage. Almost immediately, I noticed the way they worshiped together. Whenever we stood during service, they rose to their feet as one, with arms around each other's waists. They literally held each other up. In fact, we used to say that together they formed the letter *A* the way they leaned in together! The comfort Lee and Sylvia provided for each other was evident, in and outside church. The witness of their life in Christ brought comfort to others too.

LEAN BACK:

Who could use some comfort from you today? Your shoulder to lean on? Go ahead, allow that someone to lean on you.

STIR UP ONE ANOTHER AND ENCOURAGE ONE ANOTHER

And let us consider how to stir up one another to love and good works, not neglecting to meet together, as is the habit of some, but encouraging one another, and all the more as you see the Day drawing near. (Hebrews 10:24–25)

ONE SIMPLE ACT

My son was home for a few days, and we'd decided to enjoy coffee and brunch together before he left. At the coffee counter, our barista, Angie, chatted with us as she took our order, then pointed to the new Gucci bars in the display below, hinting that we would love them. My mouth watered as she described their taste, but we politely declined, picked up our order, and settled into a booth.

My son removed his cap, and we bowed our heads to pray, thanking God for the food, the barista, and the talk time ahead. While we were eating, Angie appeared, plate in hand along with a handwritten note that said, "We admire that you prayed before your meal. Please enjoy this complimentary Gucci bar. God bless you." She placed them on the table, smiled broadly, and said, "Thank you!"

We hadn't considered that anyone was watching as we prayed, and we were humbled by her generous appreciation. She went on to say that one simple act can impact other customers who notice too. She thanked us for being living witnesses for Christ.

As I share this story, I don't seek attention for my son or myself, or to the fact that we prayed in public, but I share it to honor Angie, who glorified God, and to encourage you:

- ❤ Engage in friendly conversation with those who serve you in every situation.

- ❤ Wear and share your faith, not for the attention of others, but as a living witness and with intentional response to God's provision and blessings.

- ❤ Stir up others, as Angie did that day!

WHO DO YOU LEAN INTO? REACH OUT TO ME!

My friend Darci is a dynamo mom with armfuls of blessings, but there are days she needs a listening ear and a word of encouragement. Accepting her emotions and leaning into those she trusts makes all the difference. Darci shared,

> Do you ever feel like you might not be in the right profession? Like you just aren't supposed to be doing the job you are doing? You aren't cut out for it and need to find a new path? Sometimes these feelings last a few hours, sometimes a day, sometimes weeks, months, or even years.
>
> Today I did not feel like being a stay-at-home mom was meant for me. I wasn't enough for the kids, my house was a disaster in every room, and I was just tired and wasn't enjoying the day like I wanted to with my kids.
>
> For me it only lasted a few hours, but my husband encouraged me and supported me through those feelings. Something I've learned recently is that you have to let yourself sit in the negative emotions and accept them. I am not saying dwell on them for extended amounts of time,

LEANING-IN ACTION: Surprise someone with a gift or note of appreciation. Be intentional. Follow through when nudged..

Encourage one another. You'll be so glad you did. And God will be praised!

but when I allow myself to have those feelings and lean in to those I trust, I notice that I move past them in a much healthier way. Life isn't easy. Who do you lean into? If you can't think of anyone, you can always reach out to me.[53]

When you're in need of encouragement, consider reaching out to someone else who could use some leaning time too. On the same day Darci felt this way, she penned this piece and ended it by generously offering others to lean into her. Even a small gesture can make a significant difference to the recipient!

LEAN BACK:
Whom do you lean into? Who might reach out to you for some mutual leaning? How could you lift up someone today? Maybe you could share a video call or a coffee break. Take a day trip to do something you both enjoy. What will you do?

Serve ONE ANOTHER

Through love serve one another. (Galatians 5:13)

When our twins were in kindergarten, my husband and I were volunteers for our church's youth ministry. Our kids loved serving alongside us at several youth events, and they did so with all the enthusiasm of a couple five-year-olds! Month after month, they served food, sang praises, cleaned event spaces, and more.

The following summer, while our family was away from the house, the youth group created a surprise thank-you by forking our yard and chalking our driveway. When we approached our home, we spied 1,000 white plastic forks poking out of the lawn, tines up. Then we saw our names written beside Bible verses and words of thanks, chalked decoratively up and down the driveway. We told the twins to look out the car window. As soon as we stopped, our son jumped out, gasped, fell into fits of giggles, then ran up and down the sidewalk shouting, "We're famous! We're famous!" He didn't really understand fame, but he knew that our youth group, whom we served in love, had just served us in a special way too. My son's response revealed his joy; he felt known, seen, honored, and loved.

"Whatever you do, work heartily, as for the Lord and not for men. . . . You are serving the Lord Christ" (Colossians 3:23–24). Our children were just beginning to use their gifts to serve others, and their joy was evident. They were truly serving "heartily," and I believe the members of our youth group saw Jesus in them. He was glorified in our children's service, and in that of the youth group, who served us right back!

> **As each has received a gift, use it to serve one another, as good stewards of God's varied grace. (1 Peter 4:10)**

EVEN MORE "ONE ANOTHERS!"

LEANING-IN
ACTION: Assume
a leaning posture
today as you
serve someone.
What will you do
to humbly place
this person's
needs ahead
of your own?
How might you
thank someone
for their humble
service to you?

LEAN IN #1: Here's a fun fact: both Paul and James provide us with instructions concerning how not to lean. What directives are in these verses? Which is particularly difficult for you? Confess it to the Lord, receive His grace, and seek His help. Lean on Him.

Romans 14:13

Galatians 5:15

Galatians 5:26

Colossians 3:9

James 4:11

James 5:9

LEAN IN #2: The "one anothers" we've studied are only a portion of the many exhortations in the New Testament. Which are found in the following verses? Choose three that stand out to you and write or talk about them. How can you, by God's grace, live out these "one anothers" in specific situations? With joy, in response to Christ's saving work in you, by the Holy Spirit's limitless power!

Mark 9:50; 2 Corinthians 13:11

John 13:14

Romans 12:10

Romans 12:16; Romans 15:5

Romans 15:7

Romans 16:16; 1 Peter 5:14

1 Corinthians 12:25

Ephesians 4:2; Colossians 3:13

Ephesians 5:19

Ephesians 5:21

1 Thessalonians 5:15

1 John 1:7

1 Peter 4:9

1 Peter 5:5

A Few Last "One Another" Thoughts . . .

Boundaries

I welcome people to lean on me. But I don't want to pretend I can support too much weight. I have been known to spread myself so thin that I can't offer the kind of care I'd like to give. While I would love to personally serve, lean in, and listen to dozens of people, I cannot. And that's hard for me to admit.

There are rigorous seasons when we might feel especially stretched. When that happens, we would be wise to establish healthy boundaries and take enough time with the Lord to be refueled so we can serve again.

One-Way Leaning

Quid pro quo isn't the standard for every relationship. We can't simply say, "I have allowed you to lean on me, so now it's my turn to lean on you." Every relationship is unique. Some lean primarily one way. Great examples are a mentor and mentee, parents and children, or a teacher and students. That said, even these relationships change over time. Many teachers have told me their former students grew up to be leaders in the community, and the teachers now lean on those they once taught. My relationships with my children have changed as they've grown into outstanding adults. We lean on one another now too!

LEAN BACK:
Time with the Lord is the greatest reason we set boundaries. What other reasons can you think of?

Trust that God is working through others; receive His embrace through theirs; believe that He works through you too.

Leaning on Others

When has something in life hit you unawares, knocking you off your feet? Who has God provided in the past to come alongside you, lift you up, and encourage you? "Therefore encourage one another and build one another up, just as you are doing" (1 Thessalonians 5:11).

What's your need today? Are you in need of prayer regarding health, finances, or relationships? Do you need hands-on support regarding a temptation you're facing or battling? Maybe you need advice for future education or work possibilities. Or perhaps your burdens lead you to need tangible assistance like a ride, a meal, or a grocery delivery. How can you humbly welcome and receive help?

When we humble ourselves to lean on others in our times of need, we bless them too. We allow them to honor God in their service and in their prayers for us as they use their gifts.

In challenging times, in joy-filled times—at ALL times—we need one another; we are surrounded by God's care and His grace through His people. We lean on Jesus, and we lean on one another. We receive His embrace, and we receive theirs too.

LEAN BACK:

How have or can you connect with another person when you are in a moment or season of weakness?

Lean in Together
AND LEAN ON JESUS

We receive all that we need from the Lord: forgiveness
and strength for today, direction for today and tomorrow,
and hope for eternity. We lean on Him and follow His lead
as He calls us into each vocation and into one another's
lives. We need Him first *and* we need one another. Let's
lean in together and lean on Jesus.

WEEK ONE

DAY ONE

Lean In #1: Wording will vary; possibilities include the following: Jesus says, "Follow Me"; He is Lord and leader of our lives. We listen to His teaching and we learn at His feet. He knows and provides for our needs as we trust in Him. We rely fully on Him for salvation for eternity and strength for today.

Lean In #2: "He will carry them in His bosom" = He shall fold me to His breast.

"He will gather the lambs in His arms" = There within His arms to rest.

Lean In #3: Psalm 23:1–3—For my Shepherd gently guides me, Knows my need and well provides me; Isaiah 43:1 and John 10:3—Even calls me by my name; Jeremiah 31:3 and 1 John 3:1a—Loves me ev'ry day the same; John 10:14—I am Jesus' little lamb, Ever glad at heart I am.

DAY TWO

Lean In #1: He took them in His arms and laid His hand on them; He did not refuse them; rather, He eagerly received them; He blessed the children. Jesus wants us to trust Him fully, to recognize our complete dependence on Him, like that of a little child and her trusted parent.

Lean In #2: Suggestions for shapes or emojis that take the shape of love: John 3:16—a heart and the earth; John 14:2–3—a house and light streaming from clouds; Ephesians 3:16–19—a heart with plant roots, a strong arm, and arrows extending outward in all four directions; a heart with a cross; a greater-than symbol with a brain; an overflowing cup.

Lean In #3: Isaiah 49:15—a woman who could not forget her nursing child; Isaiah 62:5—a bridegroom rejoicing over his bride; Luke 13:34—a hen gathering her brood under her wings; Luke 15:11–32—a father welcoming his prodigal son with open arms and a celebration upon his return; John 15:13—someone who lays down his life for his friends, so great is his love for them.

DAY THREE

Lean In #1a: Next to the wisdom of God, the wisdom of the world is foolishness (v. 20). "The foolishness of God is wiser than men" (v. 25). The wisdom of God is found in the message of the cross—in Christ crucified (v. 23). "Christ the power of God and the wisdom of God" (v. 24). Jesus "became to us wisdom from God" (v. 30). By faith in "Christ . . . the wisdom of God," we receive redemption, sanctification, and righteousness.

1b: We can apply this passage for guidance in daily decision-making, remembering that God's wisdom is incomparably greater than the world's wisdom. Our faith in Christ can lead every decision we make. We would not seek worldly wisdom that does not acknowledge God; ultimately, worldly wisdom is foolishness. The decisions we make won't make sense to a watching world but can provide a consistent witness for Christ.

Lean In #2: Psalm 139:1–3, 13—He knows everything about you; He perceives your thoughts; He formed you in your mother's womb; Isaiah 45:12—He created the heavens, the earth, and mankind; Matthew 10:29–31—He knows the number of hairs on your head; Matthew 28:20b—He is with you always; Acts 1:9–11—Jesus is lifted up into heaven (ascended); 1 Corinthians 15:3–4—Christ died for your sins and rose on the third day; Colossians 1:27—Christ lives in you; 2 Timothy 3:16—All Scripture is breathed out by God; it's His inspired Word; Hebrews 4:12a—God's Word is living and active; Revelation 1:8—He is "the Alpha and the Omega . . . who is and who was and who is to come."

DAY FOUR

Lean In #1: God is righteous; a rock of refuge; my rock and my fortress; my hope, my trust.

Lean In #2: Significant words repeated: refuge, rescue, save, rock. Refuge and rock speak to the protection and strength of the Lord, who is worthy of trust and able to rescue and save. Similar words: trust and leaned. Personal words: You (the Lord) and I (the psalmist) throughout the psalm; inclined, leaned, You . . . took me from my mother's womb.

DAY FIVE

Lean In #1: Christ in us by the Holy Spirit; Christ is revealed in us.

Lean In #2: 1 Timothy—Jesus was revealed (manifested) in the flesh. 1 Peter—Though He was with God in the beginning "before the foundation of the world," He came in the flesh (was made manifest) for our sake, because it's through Him that we believe in God and have hope. 1 John—John and others heard, saw, and touched God in the flesh—the Word of life—and they testified to it and proclaimed eternal life in the One who was revealed in the flesh (made manifest). God's love was revealed (made manifest) among His people by sending His Son to us so we might live through Him.

WEEK TWO

DAY ONE

Lean In #1: The one who trusts in the name of the Lord is the one who relies on God. The person who relies on God will walk in light and no longer in darkness. In trust, he will fear the Lord and obey the Word, as spoken through Isaiah, God's servant.

Lean In #2: "And we know that for those who love God all things work together for good, for those who are called according to His purpose" (Romans 8:28).

DAY TWO

Lean In #1: Inclining your heart to . . . (2:2); finds wisdom and . . . gets . . . (3:13); incline your ear to . . . (5:1); keeps . . . (19:8); buy . . . (23:23).

Lean In #2: We receive "the Spirit who is from God, that we might understand the things freely given us by God" (v. 12). The only way we can understand the truth of God and His Word is by faith through the Spirit. "The natural person"—a person without faith—will not understand or receive things that are only spiritually discerned. To have "the mind of Christ" is to have spiritual insight and understanding through faith in the Gospel of Christ.

Lean In #3: Wording will vary, but may include the following: (top three rows) our ways are not always right; our hearts can deceive us; (middle three rows) we change our minds; our feelings fluctuate; (bottom three rows) our understanding is limited; we cannot see fully, as God can.

DAY THREE

Lean In #1: When the Jews saw Jesus weeping, some remarked how He loved Lazarus. Others wondered why He couldn't have kept Lazarus from dying. We can imagine Mary's feelings of deep grief, as she fell at Jesus' feet and by what she said. Jesus was "deeply moved in His spirit and greatly troubled" (v. 33). He wept, expressing His own sorrow over death. He was "deeply moved again" (v. 38). Additional thoughts will be unique to each person.

Lean In #2: Answers will be unique to each person and may include more than one or all of the possibilities listed, in addition to others.

DAY FOUR

Lean In #1: He asks Jesus to help (drive out the evil spirit), saying, "If You can . . . ." And Jesus said to him, "'If You can'! All things are possible for one who believes" (v. 23). The father does believe, but perhaps because of his overwhelming circumstances, he has doubts too. He cries out, asking for greater faith. Today, as then, believers ask for God's help or healing, but we may hesitate in our weakness of faith. Maybe our circumstances have led us to believe there's little hope. Led by the Spirit, we confess our lack of faith and ask for greater faith too.

Lean In #2: King David found himself in a pit of destruction—in a miry bog. He waited for the Lord; he cried out for help. The Lord inclined (leaned!) toward David; He heard his cry; He drew David up, set him on solid ground, and made his steps secure. In my trials, I can cry to God, confident that He inclines to me (He is near me; He leans in); He hears me and helps me. He leads me to sing His praises! I have a new song—a new reason to praise my Lord!

trust in the Lord because He IS the rock upon which we stand; our steps are secure. Isaiah's words resound as praise and also serve as a call to trust.

Lean In #3: Isaiah proclaims complete

DAY FIVE

Lean In #1: You should be anxious about nothing; you can pray about everything. Bring your requests before the Lord with thanksgiving! He trades your anxiety for His peace, even when it makes no sense to us or to anyone else that we could possibly possess peace in the middle of uncertain circumstances. It's ours by faith in Christ, who puts a guard of protection over our

hearts and minds.

Lean In #2: We receive fellowship, joy, blessings, peace, safety and security, a light for our path, nothing to fear, and the Lord's presence. The second verse speaks of walking on a path that grows brighter day by day, thus the path is clear. Proverbs 3:6 says the Lord will "make straight your paths."

WEEK THREE

DAY ONE

Lean In #1: John 14:27—Christ's peace, which He gives to us by faith, is unlike anything the world attempts to offer; we have no need to fear. Revelation 14:13—John hears a voice from heaven, telling him that those who die in the Lord—those who remain faithful— will enter eternal rest with the Lord. 1 Peter 5:10—The God of grace who has called us in Christ will restore, confirm, strengthen, and establish us.

Lean In #2: Jesus went by Himself to be with the Father—to pray alone, sometimes up on a mountain, a desolate place. We read that He rose early to pray alone; other times, He prayed all night. He encouraged His disciples to come away to a desolate place to rest. He knew they needed rest from the rigorous teaching and healing ministry too. They left in a boat, seeking a desolate place.

DAY TWO

Lean In #1: Answers will vary but may include the following: Rest in the shadow of the Almighty. Submit to His authority; He is Lord of your life! Expect that He will lift you up

Lean In #2: Answers will be unique to each person. Remember that surrender is all about letting go, resting in His grace, and receiving His peace.

DAY THREE

Lean In #1: 2 Chronicles 30:8—Yield, serve; to come into His consecrated (sacred) sanctuary is to come in humility, yielded to His lordship. Psalm 55:22—Cast, sustain; we humbly cast our burdens onto Him who is mighty to sustain us. James 4:10—Humble; only the One who is truly exalted can lift up (exalt) us.

Lean In #2: These verses share many fruits the Holy Spirit produces in us by faith. Trust God to work in your life, by the power of the Spirit, enabling you to bear fruit and practice each of these, even self-control.

DAY FOUR

Lean In #1: Answers will vary but may include the following: I can place my complete trust in God, not in myself or limited understanding; I acknowledge Him as Lord and leader of my life. I humble myself under His protective care, casting my anxieties on the One who cares for me. He goes before me and walks beside me; I don't need to fear. I can let go and let God.

Lean In #2: You are freed from the law of sin and death. You walk according to the Spirit and set your mind on the things of the Spirit, which are life and peace. Because the Spirit of Christ lives in you, you receive His righteousness by faith; you belong to Him. Because the Spirit of the One who raised Jesus from the dead lives in you, He will raise you from the dead too!

DAY FIVE

Lean In #1: By Christ's death and resurrection, He set His people free from slavery to sin and death. The old laws included circumcision, and some Jewish converts, the Judaizers, were demanding it in the Galatian Church. Christ set people free from the yoke of the Law. By insisting upon circumcision, they would be obligated to keep the whole law, the burdensome yoke that He'd lifted already. Only by faith in Christ, through the Spirit, are people saved.

Lean In #2: The same One who was "pierced for our transgressions" (Isaiah 53:5) is the One who "bore our sins in His body" (1 Peter 2:24). Peter proclaims what Isaiah prophesied: "by His wounds you have been healed"; "with His wounds we are healed."

WEEK FOUR

DAY ONE

Lean In #1: Strength—God gives power and strength. He increases and renews the strength of the weak. He strengthens us with power through His Spirit so that Christ may live in us, and so that we may know the fullness of His love. He supplies strength to serve.

Courage—Courage comes from the Lord, who goes with us and will never leave us. He preserves the faithful and provides courage while we wait on Him. We don't have to fear because He is with us; our God will strengthen, help, and uphold us. We don't need to be troubled or afraid; He gives us His peace.

Determination—The Lord determines our steps. We make plans, but the Lord's purpose stands. Because we have the victory through Christ, we are steadfast and immovable. God fulfills our resolve for good and our works of faith by His power.

Perseverance—By the Holy Spirit, we can endure/persevere in our sufferings. We stand firm, persevering in the Lord in the strength of His might, covered with the armor of God. By His power, we are strengthened to endure. By faith, we run with endurance, looking to Jesus, the One who founded our faith, the One who endured the cross and endured hostility so that we may endure (not grow weary or fainthearted).

Lean In #2: Answers will be specific to each person. Suggestions include the following:

It's possible that what you are sure you want isn't what is best for you. "No limits" is vague and unrealistic. Achieving can be a great thing, but is "wanting it" a strong reason, alone, to go after it? Alternate: "Go for excellence, by His grace and for His glory!"

Am I a failure if I don't feel strong or courageous some days? No. I battle fear too. Alternate: "In Christ, I am strong and courageous, and I need not fear!"

Some things are beyond my control to change, even with the most positive outlook. Alternate: "The power of Christ in me compels me to make the most of my today!"

I'm wary because this and other claims like it are all about me. My dream may be self-serving. Alternate: "I have great expectations that He 'who is able to do far more abundantly than all that [I] ask or think, according to the power at work within [me], to Him be glory' (Ephesians 3:20–21)."

DAY TWO

Lean In #1: We are sinners; in humility we are teachable. We are weak and needy. In our weakness, sometimes we don't know what to pray for. In His goodness, God instructs, leads, and teaches; He has pity on us and saves us—Christ died for us. He helps; He intercedes by the Spirit.

Lean In #2: Safe in the salvation = helmet; covered with Christ's righteousness =

breastplate; surrounded by His truth = belt; ready to run with the Gospel of peace = shoes; faith defending us = shield; living and active Word = sword of the Spirit, the Word of God.

Lean In #3: Ephesians 3—Christ lives in your heart by faith; you are rooted and grounded in love, the love of Christ. Colossians 2—You are rooted and built up in Christ, established in the faith. Rooted in love (in the love of Christ) = Rooted in Christ.

DAY THREE

Lean In #1: Ephesians 3:20—The Lord does immeasurably more than we can imagine, by His power at work within us. Philippians 1:6—The Creator of our faith—the One who began a good work in us—will bring it to completion when Jesus returns. Philippians 2:13—He continues His good work in us, according to His will and for His good pleasure. James 1:17—God is the giver of every good and perfect gift.

Lean In #2: In his weakness, the power of Christ rested upon him; Christ was the source of his strength. We ourselves are weak; in Christ, we are strong!

Lean In #3: 2 Corinthians 3:4–6—We cannot claim sufficiency on our own; only in God are we sufficient to share Christ (to be ministers of a new covenant); He works through us. 9:8—By His abundant grace, He has made us sufficient so that we "may abound in every good work." 12:9–10—His grace is sufficient; His power is displayed in our weakness.

DAY FOUR

Lean In #1: Rock, fortress, deliverer, refuge, shield, horn of salvation, stronghold. With these words, you can envision a place of protection or a towering wall. The Lord inclines His ear (leans in and listens); He rescues, saves, leads, guides, and loves.

Lean In #2: What or who surrounds others: You (the Lord), steadfast love, mountains, the Lord. Who is being surrounded: me (David, the psalmist, and all believers), the one who trusts in the Lord, Jerusalem, His people.

DAY FIVE

Lean In #1: Luke 13—A disabled woman was bent over and could not straighten herself. Jesus spoke to her and told her she was freed from her disability, then He laid His hands on her and she was healed. Luke 18—A blind beggar called out to Jesus to have mercy on him. Jesus had him brought near and recovered the man's sight, commending him that his faith had made him well. Matthew 8—A leper humbly approached Jesus, who extended His hand to touch the leper, and immediately, he was cleansed. Mark 5—A man was being tortured by an unclean spirit and Jesus cast it out, sending the legion of demons into a herd of pigs. Luke 7—A sinful woman approached Jesus in repentance; weeping at His feet, she washed them with her tears and anointed His feet with ointment. Jesus forgave her sins, telling her that her faith had saved her. Mark 5—An unclean woman who had hemorrhaged for twelve years courageously touched Jesus' garment, and she was immediately healed. Jesus stopped, called her out, and commended her faith, even calling her "Daughter" (v. 34).

Lean In #2: The Lord helps, shelters (in the shadow of His wings), upholds, inclines, hears, draws up, makes steps secure (set my feet upon a rock); He is my strength and my portion; He provides a rock-steady foundation in Christ. We can remember Him and meditate on Him, sing for joy, cling to Him, wait for Him, hear His words and follow them—build our house on the Rock, on Christ.

WEEK FIVE

DAY ONE

Lean In #1: He is with you and will uphold you with His righteous right hand; His hand shall lead you and hold you.

Lean In #2: Yet (as if to say, "still" or "even then") Habakkuk will rejoice in the Lord; he will take joy in the God of his salvation; God is his strength! Shadrach, Meshach, and Abednego trust God to save them from certain death in the fiery furnace, "but if not" (even if He doesn't), they will not bow down to an idol. They remain faithful to the One they serve and trust.

DAY TWO

Lean In #1: God's actions: The Lord goes with you; He will not leave you nor forsake you; He goes before you. He will come with vengeance; He will come and save you. There is no God besides Him; there is no other Rock. He loved us and gave us eternal comfort and good hope through grace; He comforts our hearts and establishes them in every good work and word. How you can respond: Be strong and courageous; do not fear or be in dread of them; do not be dismayed. Be strong; fear not! Fear not, nor be afraid.

Lean In #2: "Jesus is on the throne!"—Colossians 3:1 and Hebrews 8:1; "God is good!"—Psalm 100:5 and Lamentations 3:25; "His Word is true!"—Ephesians 1:13 and James 1:18

DAY THREE

Lean In #1: He is so near, He has us in His hands, such that nothing can snatch us from Him.

Lean In #2: Takeaways will be unique to each person but may include the following: Grace says you are justified by the gift of God's grace, through redemption in Jesus. Comfort says God comforts you in all your afflictions so you can comfort others with the same comfort you've received. Hope says you are born again to a living hope by God's mercy through Jesus' resurrection from the dead.

DAY FOUR

Lean In #1: Answers will be unique to each person's pain and past experience. Perhaps it will draw you closer to the Lord, to see your need for Him, to see His hand more clearly.

Lean In #2: God has taught/revealed many comforting truths to Tamara: I have worth through Him. He is my purpose. He is with me. He helps me. I matter. I am more than my pain, more than my disabilities. He makes me whole. He guides me. He has control. He holds me.

DAY FIVE

Lean In #1: God created you; He formed you; He has redeemed you; He has called you by name, you are His. He is with you; He won't let the rivers overwhelm you or the fire burn you or flames consume you. You are precious in His eyes; He honors you; He loves you. He has saved you.

Lean In #2: Jesus is the way, the truth, and the life; no one comes to the Father except through Him. Even if we are faithless, He remains faithful. He is continually with me; He holds my hand. The Lord delivers me. Applications will be unique to each person.

WEEK SIX

DAY ONE

Lean In #1: The sheep follow the shepherd as he leads them out and goes before them. Jesus compares this relationship to His relationship with the Father. The shepherd lays down his life for the sheep. Jesus, the Good Shepherd, foretells His sacrificial death for the sake of His people.

Lean In #2: Mark 5:34—Jesus called the bleeding woman "Daughter." She was an outcast because she was considered unclean. Luke 10:41—He spoke Martha's name twice out of empathy; He associated with women, which was uncommon for a rabbi/teacher. Luke 19:5—He called out to Zacchaeus, a cheating tax collector, despised by his people. John 11:43—He called Lazarus to come out of the grave, the friend for whom Jesus had just wept. John 1:42 and 21:17—Jesus told Simon he would be called Cephas (Peter), which means "rock." Jesus knows and calls all people by name, whether or not they are recognized or rejected by others. He healed the bleeding woman, tenderly rebuked Martha, redeemed cheating Zacchaeus, raised Lazarus, and chose (and later, reinstated) Peter. He provides each of us with exactly what we need.

DAY TWO

Lean In #1: Law, testimonies, precepts, statutes, commandments, rules, word. (You may find slight variances, depending on the translation you use.)

Lean In #2: Verses chosen will vary.

DAY THREE

Lean In #1: Martha learned that the one thing necessary—of upmost importance—is to sit at Jesus' feet and learn from Him; she was welcome there too. She learned that He knew her heart because He acknowledged how she felt, and with His repetition of her name, He was speaking tenderly to her, with affection.[54] In that, she learned more about His care for her too.

Lean In #2: In all three instances, they "knelt down and prayed." (Matthew 26:39 says Jesus "fell on His face and prayed"; Mark 14:35 reads, "fell on the ground and prayed.") Circumstances: Jesus, in the garden just before His arrest; Peter, before the bed of a dead woman whom God raised; Paul, in an emotional farewell to the Ephesian elders. Jesus prayed in anguish; He knew He was about to take the weight of the world's sin to the cross. Peter may have assumed this posture because he was kneeling over a bed, praying for the person on it. Perhaps Paul went to his knees in fervent prayer filled with emotion amid his difficult good-bye.

DAY FOUR

Lean In #1: Power words or phrases: straining forward, press on (for the prize), run that you may obtain (the prize), run with endurance, looking to Jesus. Summarizations will vary, but may include the following: The race is set before you; it's a long one, so run with endurance. Give it all you have and don't look back. Strain forward with your eyes on the prize—the call of God in Christ.

Lean In #2: The psalmist is afflicted; he needs strength. He knows the Lord will answer when he calls. He needs rescue, a rock of refuge, a strong fortress to save him. He is poor and needy; he needs saving. Needs will be unique to each person.

DAY FIVE

Lean In #1: Colossians 2:6-7—Your identity is rooted and centered in Christ. Romans 8:14-16—You're a child of God, adopted in Christ Jesus, and that makes you an heir of the Kingdom. John 15:15—Jesus calls you His friend! Romans 12:4-5—You are a member of the Body of Christ. Acts 17:28—In Him you live and move and have your being; you are His offspring.

Lean In #2: Ephesians 1:3–14 says you are chosen, holy and blameless, adopted, redeemed, forgiven, lavished with His grace, knowledgeable of the mystery of His will, united in Him, an heir (a recipient of a future inheritance), sealed with the Holy Spirit.

WEEK SEVEN

DAY ONE

Lean In #1: We belong to the One who gave us His Spirit. "Do you not know that your body is a temple of the Holy Spirit within you, whom you have from God? You are not your own" (1 Corinthians 6:19).

Lean In #2: Together, we show honor to one another, serve the Lord with zeal and fervency, rejoice in hope, remain patient in trials, and pray constantly. Together, we contribute to others' needs and show hospitality. Together, we bless those who persecute us; we live in harmony, not haughtily, but humbly (not wise in our own sight), associating with everyone. Together, we do what is honorable because God is glorified when we do.

DAY TWO

Lean In: Circle: prophecy, service, teaching, exhortation, contributes, leads, does acts of mercy; service, activities; speaks, serves. Highlight: Spirit, Lord, God, Jesus Christ. Purposes: providing prophecy, service, instruction, exhortation (encouragement), contributions (financially and otherwise), leadership, acts of mercy, activities, leadership through speaking, and so on. Who benefits: others, one another. Who gets the glory: God through Jesus Christ.

DAY THREE

Lean In #1: Answers will vary but may include the following: We are all called to grow, as part of the body; we are joined and held together, so it's necessary for each part to work properly for the whole body to function. When we work together, the body grows; it is built up in love. Because we are one body, when one part of the body suffers, the entire body suffers; when one part is honored, the entire body rejoices.

Lean In #2: We might claim it was less efficient, but Jesus knew it was necessary that they serve together, for mutual encouragement and possibly for protection too. Nothing is wasted in God's economy.

DAY FOUR

Lean In #1: God's actions and demeanor: He opposes the proud; He gives grace to the humble. He protects you by His mighty hand. He exalts you. He cares for you. He has called you to His eternal glory. He will restore, confirm, strengthen, and establish you. Your actions/responses: clothe yourselves with humility; humble yourself under His hand. Cast your anxieties on Him. Be sober-minded and watchful. Resist the devil in your faith; know that others suffer for their faith too.

Lean In #2: Answers and application will be unique to each person.

DAY FIVE

Lean In #1: Acts 12:12—An angel has just released Peter from prison, and he comes to the house where believers have gathered together to pray for him. Romans 15:30—Paul asks believers to "strive together" in prayer for him, for protection in his travels and as he continues to serve. 1 Corinthians 1:2—Paul writes to the Church in Corinth who are "called to be saints together with all" people in all places who believe in Jesus, "both their Lord and ours." All are in the same community of believers! Ephesians 2:19–22—Jews and Gentiles, formerly separated, are now one in Christ: fellow citizens and members. The "whole structure [is] being joined together . . . built together into a dwelling place for God by the Spirit."

Lean In #2: The friends "went up on the roof and let him down with his bed through the tiles into the midst before Jesus" (v. 19). Jesus saw their faith through their action, on behalf of their friend. Because Jesus not only healed the man physically but spiritually too, with the words "Man, your sins are forgiven you" (v. 20), the religious leaders charged Jesus with blasphemy (claiming to be God), even saying, "Who can forgive sins but God alone?" (v. 21). Jesus just proved their very charge—God, indeed!

WEEK EIGHT

DAY ONE

Lean In #1: Our hearts are sealed by faith with the Holy Spirit; He is our promise—our guarantee—of the inheritance that we will claim in "Thy courts above" when Christ returns. We receive comfort trusting His promise of salvation!

Lean In #2: Answers may be unique to each person. Suggestions include the following: Pray for God's guidance in your upcoming conversation; silence your phone; set time boundaries, letting your friend know in advance the time frame you can connect so you have similar expectations; schedule white space on your calendar to allow for one or two coffee-meets per week, so when your friend asks, you have options.

DAY TWO

Lean In #1: Romans 12:10—Love with brotherly affection; show honor. 1 Thessalonians 3:12—God works in you, enabling you to increase and abound in love. 1 Peter 4:8—Love earnestly; love covers a multitude of sins. 1 John 4:7-12—Love is from God, so whoever loves knows God and has been born of Him. God's love was made manifest in Christ; we live through Him. This is love: God loved us and sent His Son to pay the price for our sins. God abides in us, and His love is perfected in us as we love one another.

Lean In #2: Paul said, "Be imitators of me, as I am of Christ" (1 Corinthians 11:1). "Truly, truly, I say to you, the Son can do nothing of His own accord, but only what He sees the Father doing. For whatever the Father does, that the Son does likewise" (John 5:19). We do nothing on our own, but only as He leads. By His grace, may we join Him on His mission, following His lead.

DAY THREE

Lean In: Similar to "admonish" (which means "rebuke" or "reprimand"), you are to gently restore a fellow believer caught in sin while keeping watch on yourself, so you aren't tempted. Bear one another's burdens. Exhort (urge, spur on) one another; hold one another accountable so none of you is hardened or deceived by sin.

DAY FIVE

Lean In #1: (. . . = one another) We should not pass judgment on . . .; bite and devour or be consumed by . . .; provoke or envy . . .; lie to . . .; speak evil against . . .; grumble against . . .

Lean In #2: (. . . = one another) Be at peace with . . .; comfort . . .; agree with . . .; wash . . . feet; outdo . . . in showing honor; live in harmony with . . .; welcome . . .; greet . . . with a kiss; have the same care for . . .; bearing with . . . in love; address . . . in psalms and hymns; submitting to . . .; do good to . . .; fellowship with . . .; show hospitality to . . .; humility toward . . . . Choices will be unique to each person.

ENDNOTES

1   "I Am Jesus' Little Lamb," *Lutheran Service Book* (St. Louis: Concordia Publishing House, 2006), 740:1, 3.

2   Stephen Morris, "Domino Chain Reaction," YouTube video, October 4, 2009, https://www.youtube.com/watch?v=y97rBdSYbkg.

3   Lindsay Hausch, Facebook, January 23, 2022. Used by permission.

4   Corrie ten Boom, The Hiding Place, quoted on Goodreads, accessed August 12, 2022, https://www.goodreads.com/author/quotes/102203.Corrie_ten_Boom?page=4.

5   Justin Pot, "You Can't Pull Yourself up by Your Bootstraps," *Zapier* (blog), December 3, 2021, https://zapier.com/blog/you-cant-pull-yourself-up-by-your-bootstraps/.

6   Alli Hoff Kosik, "Self Empowerment: What It Is and How to Achieve It," *SkillShare* (blog), February 15, 2022, https://www.skillshare.com/blog/self-empowerment-what-it-is-and-how-to-achieve-it/.

7   John Stonestreet and Maria Baer, "'The Whisper Method' Recycles Old, Bad Ideas," Breakpoint Colson Center (website), August 30, 2022, https://breakpoint.org/the-whisper-method-recycles-old-bad-ideas/.

8   Stonestreet and Baer, "'The Whisper Method' Recycles Old, Bad Ideas."

9   Elle Hunt, "Is 'Manifesting' Dangerous Magical Thinking or a Formula for Success?" The Guardian (website), April 21, 2022, https://www.theguardian.com/lifeandstyle/2022/apr/21/is-mainfesting-real-the-secret.

10 Stonestreet and Baer, "'The Whisper Method' Recycles Old, Bad Ideas."

11 Stonestreet and Baer, "'The Whisper Method' Recycles Old, Bad Ideas."

12 *The Lutheran Study Bible* (St. Louis: Concordia Publishing House, 2009), 1079.

13 *The Lutheran Study Bible* (St. Louis: Concordia Publishing House, 2009), 2166 (note on 1 Peter 3:10).

14 Andrew E. Steinmann, *Proverbs*, Concordia Commentary (St. Louis: Concordia Publishing House, 2009), 114–15.

15 Brown, Driver, Briggs, and Gesenius, *The NAS Old Testament Hebrew Lexicon*, s.v. "Sha'an," as found on Bible Study Tools (website), accessed July 15, 2022, https://www.biblestudytools.com/lexicons/hebrew/nas/shaan-2.html.

16 *Hebrew Lexicon*, s.v. "batach," as found on Bible Study Tools (website), accessed July 15, 2022, https://www.biblestudytools.com/lexicons/hebrew/nas/batach.html.

17 Steinmann, 558.

18 John Gill, *Exposition of the Bible*, as found on Bible Study Tools (website), accessed July 20, 2022, https://www.biblestudytools.com/commentaries/gills-exposition-of-the-bible/1-corinthians-13-12.html and Bible Hub (website), accessed July 20, 2022, https://biblehub.com/lexicon/1_corinthians/13-12.htm.

19 Steinmann, 435.

20 Steinmann, 115, 258, 259.

21 Deb Burma, *Raising Godly Girls* (St. Louis: Concordia Publishing House, 2015), 144.

22 Dale A. Meyer, *Timely Reflections: A Minute a Day with Dale Meyer* (Anaheim Hills, CA: Tri-Pillar Publishing, 2014), 199. Timely Reflections © 2014 by Dale A. Meyer. Used with permission. www.tripillarpublishing.com.

23 Deb Burma, *Stepping Out* (St. Louis: Concordia Publishing House, 2013), 28.

24 Kip Anderson, Facebook, November 7, 2021. Used with permission.

25 Heather J. Weber, "April 27," *Portals of Prayer*, vol. 85, no. 455 (St. Louis: Concordia Publishing House, 2022).

26 Burma, *Raising Godly Girls*, 84.

27 Debbie Larson, "It's All about Who's in Control," *Lutheran Women in Mission* (blog), April 4, 2022,

28 Burma, *Stepping Out*, 178–79.

29 Steinmann, 358.

30 Michael Eschelbach, *The Big Book of New Testament Questions and Answers* (St. Louis; Concordia Publishing House, 2015), 64.

31 Andrea Lee, "Overcoming the Illusion of Self-Sufficiency," Radical (website), November 13, 2018, https://radical.net/article/overcoming-illusion-self-sufficiency/.

32 Lee, "Overcoming the Illusion of Self-Sufficiency."

33 Sharla Fritz, *God's Relentless Love* (St. Louis: Concordia Publishing House, 2020), 115.

34 *The Lutheran Study Bible* (St. Louis: Concordia Publishing House, 2009), 1594 (note on Matthew 8:11).

35 *The Lutheran Study Bible* (St. Louis: Concordia Publishing House, 2009), 1809 (note on John 13:23).

36 *The Lutheran Study Bible* (St. Louis: Concordia Publishing House, 2009), 1780.

37 Joseph Thayer, *Greek-English Lexicon of the New Testament*, s.v. "Chorizo," as found on Bible Study Tools (website), accessed August 12, 2022, https://www.biblestudytools.com/lexicons/greek/nas/chorizo.html.

38 Sharla Fritz, *Enough for Now: Unpacking God's Sufficiency* (St. Louis: Concordia Publishing House, 2019), 86.

39 Deb Burma, *Be Still and Know: A Study of Rest and Refuge* (St. Louis: Concordia Publishing House, 2021), 159.

40 Fritz, *Enough for Now*, 99–100.

41 Lindsay Hausch, *Take Heart: God's Comfort for Anxious Thoughts* (St. Louis: Concordia Publishing House, 2021), 99.

42 Tamara Witt, comment on Deb Burma, "At what times have you most clearly recognized your need to lean on Jesus?" Facebook, June 28, 2022. Used with permission.

43 George Bruick, Facebook, August 21, 2021. Used with permission.

44 Meyer, *Timely Reflections*, 287. Note: Timely Reflections © 2014 by Dale A. Meyer. Used with permission. www.tripillarpublishing.com.

45 Hausch, *Take Heart*, 98.

46 Heidi Goehmann, *Emotions and the Gospel* (St. Louis: Concordia Publishing House, 2022), 13.

47 Burma, *Raising Godly Girls*, 48.

48 Stephen J. Carter, *Witness to the Light* (St. Louis: Concordia Publishing House, 2006), August 25 devotion.

49 Rehema Kavugha, Facebook, April 20, 2021. Used with permission.

50 Lindsay Hausch, Facebook, May 20, 2022. Used with permission.

51 "Come Thou Fount of Every Blessing," *Lutheran Service Book* (St. Louis: Concordia Publishing House, 2006), 686:3.

52 Burma, *Raising Godly Girls*, 143–44.

53 Darci Fraker, Facebook, May 11, 2021. Used with permission.

54 *The Lutheran Study Bible* (St. Louis: Concordia Publishing House, 2009), 1736 (note on Luke 10:41).

55 Tanner Olson (@writtentospeak), "God, I Don't Know. Amen." *Written to Speak* (blog), October 2, 2015, https://www.writtentospeak.com/blog/godidkamen. Used with permission.

56 Augustine of Hippo, quoted on Goodreads (website), accessed August 4, 2022, https://www.goodreads.com/author/quotes/6819578.Augustine_of_Hippo?page=3/.